The

HCG DIET
Gourmet Cookbook

TAMMY SKYE

Over 200 "Low Calorie" Recipes
for the "HCG Phase"

This book is dedicated to Dr. A.T.W. Simeons
who developed this amazing, phenomenal, miracle
weight loss protocol. Special thanks to Kevin Trudeau,
author of the book *"The Weight Loss Cure They
Don't Want You to Know About"* for bringing
this diet to the public. This book is also dedicated with
all my heart to my mother, Barbara, the dieters
on my online support group, and everyone out there
like me who has endlessly struggled to lose weight
and have finally found the answer they have been
searching for. I believe that this is the last diet you will
ever need. This book is for all of you who see the light
at the end of the tunnel and are making the choice
to lose weight and change your life forever.

*Those who say it can't be done
are usually interrupted by others doing it.*
— JOEL A. BARKER

TABLE OF CONTENTS

Glossary of Terms and Abbreviations

HCG — Human Chorionic Gonadotropin. A natural medication often used as a fertility treatment and researched and developed for the HCG Diet Protocol for weight loss by Dr. A.T.W. Simeons.

HHCG — Homeopathic HCG

LIW — "Last Injection Weight." The weight recorded on the last day of HCG injection. Used to monitor weight during Phase 3 (The Stabilizing Phase).

LSDW — "Last Sublingual Dose Weight" The weight recorded on the last day of HCG sublingual dosage.

VLCD — Very Low Calorie Diet. The term used to describe the 500 calorie "HCG Phase" of the diet.

IU — International Unit. A term to determine dosage of a medication. The amount of HCG to take daily during the "HCG Phase" of the diet is 125 iu to 250 iu.

SL — Sublingual. A term used to describe taking a medication under the tongue where it is absorbed by the capillaries and taken into the bloodstream. HCG or Homeopathic HCG (HHCG) can be taken this way as an alternative to injections.

SC/SQ — Subcutaneous. A term to describe an injection method just under the skin rather than into the muscle.

IM — Intramuscular. Injecting a medication directly into the muscle.

R1 — (Round 1), R2 (Round 2) etc. An abbreviation to describe multiple rounds of HCG. Helpful when there is a lot of weight to lose.

Loading — The term to describe the first two days on the HCG where it is required to eat large amounts of high fat foods in preparation for the VLCD.

Nutritional Loading — A term used to describe eating very healthy foods and supplements before and after the "HCG Phase" (also known as Phase 2 or P2) to promote optimal health.

The Phases

> **Prep and Load** — (Phase 1 or P1) Preparing for the HCG Diet and loading properly before beginning the "HCG Phase" of the diet.

> **The HCG Phase** — (Phase 2 or P2) The use of HCG in combination with a low calorie diet.

(continued)

1

The Stabilization Phase — (Phase 3 or P3) The 3 week period of a varied, normal calorie diet with the exception of starch and sugar.

The Maintenance Phase — (Phase 4 or P4), The last phase of the diet where you gradually incorporate carbohydrates back into your diet and maintain your new weight loss for life

Immunity — Immunity is a term to describe when the HCG is no longer effective and a break from the diet is needed. Symptoms are: severe hunger, weakness and fatigue, mental fogginess.

Apple Day — An "Apple Day" is a technique recommended by Dr. Simeons to break up a plateau in the "HCG Phase" of the diet. If you have had a plateau for 4 or more days, eat 6 apples during that day while drinking minimal water. Weight loss should resume the following day.

Steak Day — A steak day is used if a weight gain of 2 pounds over LIW/LSDW occurs during the "Stabilization Phase" (also known as Phase 3 or P3). The dieter must perform a steak day on the same day as the gain and eat nothing until the evening and then eat a large steak with either a large apple or raw tomato. The weight gain should be corrected by the following day.

Preface

I am so thrilled and excited to present to you the latest version of The HCG Diet Gourmet Cookbook. I first released this book as an e-book to a handful of special people in my dieter support group back in 2007. Back then, there was so little information about the HCG Diet and certainly very few recipes that were remotely palatable due to the limited ingredients demanded by the protocol. So out of sheer inspiration and perhaps a touch of desperation, the recipes and this book were born.

Since the time I first released this book, the HCG Diet (Human Chorionic Gonadotropin combined with a low calorie diet) has swept the nation and more and more people have discovered this amazing diet and are transforming their bodies and their lives. I've had the pleasure to meet and correspond with thousands of dieters who have shared their stories about how they lost 30, 50, 100, and even over 150 pounds using this program!

In my personal experience, what amazed me was the way the HCG Diet reshaped my body. The pounds and inches just seemed to melt away and I discovered throughout the "HCG Phase" I had little to no hunger, my food cravings were reduced, and I just felt so fantastic and full of energy.

As a determined HCG Dieter and a dedicated "foodie," I was utterly bored with plain chicken breast over lettuce, so I set out on a feverish quest to bring spice and excitement to otherwise very limited fare. It is the intention of this cookbook to provide flavor, ideas, and delicious low calorie recipes that are in accordance with the original Dr. Simeons HCG Diet.

It has been an incredible journey of personal transformation for me. I began my diet in May of 2007 and after two full rounds and one short course on the HCG Diet protocol I had lost a total of almost 60 pounds and am now happily enjoying life at my goal weight of 140 pounds.

To this day, I still have to pinch myself every time I look in the mirror. This journey has altered my life is countless ways. I am forever grateful that I found this diet. I wish you success and happiness in your HCG Diet journey and I hope that you will enjoy these recipes.

Why Do I Need This Book?

So many people following the HCG Diet protocol are utterly and completely bored and frustrated by the lack of variety in their meals during the restrictive "HCG Phase." The recipes in this book can help alleviate the struggle for taste and variety as dieters follow the very limited food choices allowed by the diet. Staying on track and motivated with any diet is certainly challenging, but with the HCG Diet in particular, the food choices allowed are so limited.

Can you be successful and lose weight on the HCG Diet eating simple grilled chicken and salad every day? Yes, but why be bored? Many people fail on diets due to lack of flavor and imagination in their meals. That is where this cookbook can help you. In the creation of the recipes in this cookbook, I was inspired by the flavors of the world and my own favorite comfort foods. In this cookbook, I share some of my favorite recipes for the low calorie "HCG Phase" of the HCG Diet such as savory meat dishes, chicken and seafood recipes, and even some specialty drinks and fresh fruit desserts.

The benefits I've experienced personally and heard about from other HCG dieters are incredible. From the seemingly simple act of being able to shop "off the rack" in a department store or wear a bikini in public for the first time, to dramatic changes in medical reports and blood tests. People have shared stories about how they could barely walk without getting short of breath, or having severe pain in their knees, and are now playing with their children and grandchildren in the back yard for the first time in years. Over the last two and a half years I've talked to and corresponded with so many people who have conquered obesity and lost 30, 50, 100 pounds or more. I never get tired of hearing these stories and it lifts my heart to know that the HCG Diet is changing so many lives for the better.

I hope you will enjoy renewed energy, improved nutrition, and ultimately a little "spice" in your diet as you watch your body shrink and your problem areas reshape. Make the HCG Diet part of a permanent lifestyle change as you learn proper diet and nutrition to create those lasting results long after the "HCG Phase" is over. You will be amazed at how wonderful you feel as you enjoy delicious food, improve your slow metabolism, and lose the weight permanently, ending the vicious cycle of yo-yo dieting. You can still enjoy delicious meals, lose weight, and keep it off permanently with the HCG Diet.

I wish each one of you all the success in the world and commend you for taking this step toward a healthier life. This diet is amazing and you have an exciting life full of unlimited possibilities and a slimmer healthier body ahead of you. I hope you enjoy these delicious recipes and remember to celebrate your body and your new life every single day.

My Story

I am a woman who has struggled with weight my entire life. I can tell you from personal experience that there are mechanisms involved beyond low calorie dieting and extreme physical exercise that affect our weight. The popular belief many people have of "calories in/calories out" is simply not the only factor in weight loss and obesity. I had dieted off and on my entire life and couldn't seem to lose weight even eating a mere 800 calories a day and performing hour long cardio and weight training workouts five days a week. It was an extremely frustrating and disheartening struggle to lose even a single pound despite making healthy food choices and exercising regularly. The weight always returned and I remained overweight and miserable.

As a child I began to gain weight at the onset of puberty. This was a critical time in my life. Something appeared to be wrong with my body which began to accumulate abnormal fat deposits on my hips, thighs, and buttocks. I went from 80 to 135 pounds almost overnight. I became emotionally sensitive about my weight, and noticed cellulite beginning to develop on my thighs and buttocks. My social life and high school experience suffered as a result of my weight and I became painfully shy. I went through years of sporadic dieting in my teens and early 20s, trying everything from extreme calorie restricted diets, prepackaged meals, shakes and bars, every over the counter diet pill imaginable, and still I gained. I tried low carbohydrate dieting and food combining and considered painful plastic surgery. I would have considered just about anything that would help me lose those unwanted pounds and bulges. I never lost more than 20 pounds on any of these diets and always regained every single pound and more as soon as I resumed a quasi-normal diet.

After the death of my mother six years ago, my weight soared to nearly 200 pounds. I felt depressed, out of control, and helpless to control my weight. My mother had never taken proper care of herself and ate many of the sugary, starchy foods that as a Type 1 diabetic she was supposed to control. At the age of 30 she suffered a massive heart attack requiring quadruple bypass surgery. Over the years, her health issues and poor eating habits took a toll on her heart and kidneys. I lost my mother to complications of her diabetes when she passed away at the young age of 55 years old. It was this experience that was, in a sense, the catalyst for change in my life. I realized that unless I took steps to change my weight and unhealthy eating habits that I was following in her footsteps.

After my mother's death I became obsessed with learning everything I could about health and nutrition. I delved deeply into alternative medicine studies and

> It was an extremely frustrating and disheartening struggle to lose even a single pound despite making healthy food choices and exercising regularly.

research. I studied herbs and vitamins and their effect on the human body. I began a feverish and lifelong quest to cure the source of my own obesity and other potential health issues.

I started making small changes in my lifestyle. I changed my diet to natural and organic foods. I gave up sodas and limited my exposure to starches and sugary food. I discovered the all natural herb Stevia as a sweetener alternative to the artificial sweeteners aspartame and sucralose. I experimented with various cleanses and started looking at food and nutrition as medicine. I weaned myself off of all medications including anti-depressants and over the counter pain remedies. These changes in my diet really began to improve my health in a dramatic way and I lost 10 pounds just from making these changes.

Then, one day as I struggled yet again to maintain my forever fluctuating weight, I happened to catch an infomercial on television for Kevin Trudeau's latest book, "The Weight Loss Cure They Don't Want You to Know About." I started researching study after study online to determine the protocol's safety and effectiveness. I actively looked for side-effects and any sign that the protocol could be dangerous. I spent nearly three weeks researching and I discovered that it was indeed safe and that the weight loss results were amazing and life-changing for countless people just like me. I found support groups filled with people following the diet. It was this research that led me to the original protocol published by Dr. A.T.W. Simeons at the Salvator Mundi International Hospital in Rome, Italy. The book is called *"Pounds and Inches, a New Approach to Obesity."* Dr. Simeons refined this amazing weight loss protocol over many years and treated thousands of patients successfully with HCG for the condition of obesity.

I knew undeniably that I'd finally found the answer to my weight problem. Now, at the age of 40, I am excited about life again. Life as the thin, beautiful, and healthy person I always dreamed I could be — and now I've achieved that goal.

I originally embarked on this amazing journey to cure myself of obesity and now I feel I have a personal mission to help others discover this amazing diet and share my delicious recipes. More and more people are discovering the amazing weight loss and health benefits from following the HCG Diet program and having wonderful success. I wish you all the very best and I'm here to tell you that this will quite possibly be the last diet you ever have to do to change your life forever.

About the HCG Diet

What is the HCG Diet?

The HCG Diet is a revolutionary diet using Human Chorionic Gonadotropin (HCG) combined with a low calorie diet of 500 calories a day. Taking the HCG for a period of 23 or 43 days while observing a strict, food specific, low calorie diet allows the body to burn fat at a rapid rate. While the dieter is on the HCG, the body utilizes the abnormal fat stores of the body for fuel. It is also theorized by the doctor who developed the diet, that the hypothalamus gland is reset at the end of the protocol improving the metabolism, and regulating the endocrine systems more efficiently. After the "HCG Phase" (also known as Phase 2 or P2), you can eat a normal calorie diet with a large variety of foods with the exception of starches and sugars for a period of 3 weeks I call "The Stabilization Phase" (also known as Phase 3 or P3). Finally, in the "Maintenance Phase" (also known as Phase 4 or P4) you can begin to slowly incorporate carbohydrates back into your diet and enjoy your new, faster metabolism.

History of the HCG Diet

The HCG Diet protocol was developed by Dr. A.T.W. Simeons in the 1950s when he discovered the connection between obesity and a treatment using HCG for boys who had a hormonal imbalance and were significantly overweight. He theorized and studied the use of HCG as a treatment for weight loss and found it extremely effective when done properly by correcting a metabolic disorder of the hypothalamus gland. His patients lost incredible amounts of weight and had an improved metabolism as a result of the treatment. I highly recommend reading the original book by Dr. A.T.W Simeons, *"Pounds and Inches"* for a detailed analysis of the process and how it affects the body.

The HCG Diet has experienced a resurgence since the release of Kevin Trudeau's book *"The Weight Loss Cure They Don't Want You to Know About"* which discusses in detail Dr. Simeons' original protocol with a few minor variations and other health recommendations and suggestions. The differences between Kevin Trudeau's version of the HCG Diet program and Dr. Simeons' are that Mr. Trudeau omits the use of shellfish in the diet and also the orange as a fruit choice. Otherwise, the diet is virtually the same. The recipes in this book follow the original HCG Diet developed by Dr. Simeons and do contain oranges and shellfish but can be easily modified to substitute white fish, beef or chicken, if desired.

Expected Weight Loss

Weight loss of up to one pound a day can be expected on average. Men tend to lose a little faster than women. The amount you can lose also depends on how much you have to lose and how strictly you follow the diet. If you want to lose 100 pounds or more, you will lose much more and much faster than if you only have 20 pounds to lose. It is advisable to stop the diet if more than 34 pounds have been lost or if 43 injections have been completed. People who have a lot of weight to lose can safely lose 5-6 pounds more if desired but it is advisable to transition to "The Stabilization Phase" (also known as Phase 3 or P3) when 34 pounds is reached.

Choosing a Clinic

When choosing a clinic, examine the program carefully. Make sure that it is in compliance with the original program developed by Dr. Simeons. The dosages for injections should be 125-200 iu of HCG taken once per day (a higher dosage of approximately 150 iu twice a day is required for sublingual formulations) for 6 days a week for a period of 23 or 43 days. The food choices and other restrictions should be compliant with the original protocol. You should not be required to purchase any additional supplements, shakes, or be advised to use oils on your body while on the "HCG Phase" of the program. This can slow or stall your weight loss and can often be a costly and unnecessary expense.

It is very important to choose a reputable clinic and physician to monitor you while on the program and make sure that your HCG is fresh and potent at the time you begin. When evaluating a clinic for their HCG program, consider the cost, support, and benefits they offer you. HCG, although not officially endorsed by

the FDA for weight loss is an all natural prescription medication, any open-minded doctor can write a prescription for you, and HCG is available at most pharmacies.

Multiple Rounds of HCG

If you require more than one round to reach your goal weight, you can begin another round after a period of about 6 weeks including 3 weeks on "The Stabilization Phase" (also known as Phase 3 or P3) and 3 weeks (or more) of maintenance eating. You should increase the time between rounds after 2 or more in order to prevent immunity. By following this plan and taking breaks in between rounds, it's quite possible to lose 100 pounds or more.

Immunity

Immunity to HCG can occur sometimes and is characterized by extreme hunger, feelings of weakness, and a lightheaded feeling. This is an indication that you should consider transitioning to the "The Stabilization Phase" (also known as Phase 3 or P3) and it is time to take a break. Another time you might experience immunity is when you get close to your goal weight or the ideal weight for you. To prevent immunity, it is helpful and recommended by Dr. Simeons to take one day off per week when doing a full 43 day course. If you feel you are having the symptoms of immunity, you should increase your calories

HCG DIET Tip *Taking before and after photos (front, side, back) can help you stay motivated as you track your progress with the HCG Diet as you watch your body shrink.*

of the recommended foods to 800 calories per day and complete a minimum of 23 days of injections and then transition to "The Stabilization Phase" (also known as Phase 3 or P3). The HCG will not allow you to reduce your weight too low without showing you signs of immunity so it is wise to take a break if you begin experiencing the symptoms. If you want that starved, gaunt, skinny look this is not the diet for you. The HCG Diet will however, help you achieve a normal, healthy weight for your age, height, and frame.

Exercise

It isn't recommended to exercise heavily while on the "HCG Phase" of the diet. Heavy exercise seems to cause stalls in weight loss possibly due to the water retention required by the muscles during exercise. Light exercise like walking, Yoga, stretching, and rebounding are good exercises to do. Once you transition to P3, you can start your cardio, weight lifting, and regular exercise routine if you wish.

The Abnormal Fat Loss Phenomenon

One phenomenon experienced by most HCG dieters following Dr. Simeons' protocol is the way the HCG tends to redistribute fat away from your "problem areas" or abnormal fat deposits. In my personal experience, I noticed that my hips and thighs lost the highest percentage of inches as well as significant inches lost from my stomach and waist. This phenomenon is fairly unique to the HCG Diet when compared with other weight loss

programs.

Ways to Take HCG

INJECTIONS

HCG is most commonly injected Intramuscularly (IM) and some people inject Subcutaneously (SC/SQ). The recommended dosage is 125 iu up to 200 iu and the HCG is injected daily 6 days per week for a period of 43 days or daily for a period of 23 days. It is not advisable to go higher than 200 iu daily or weight gain may occur. The HCG must be kept cold, dark, and fresh. It can last in the refrigerator for approximately 25 days.

SUBLINGUAL HCG

Since the time I first released this book the Sublingual (SL) form of the HCG Diet has become popular among dieters who are enjoying the same weight loss success as those who are injecting. The HCG is combined with a small amount of colloidal silver and sometimes some B12 which helps to facilitate the transport of the molecule into the bloodstream through the capillaries under the tongue. When taking sublingual HCG, it is necessary to take a stronger dosage (approximately 150 iu) under the tongue twice a day (morning and evening) in order to insure receiving an adequate dosage. Some clinics report that it is not necessary to take the breaks between rounds when using sublingual HCG but I strongly recommend taking them anyway. "The HCG Phase" (also known as Phase 2 or P2) is so restrictive that even if you don't experience immunity, you still need the varied nutrition and breaks to give your body a rest and insure good health.

In recent months a new form of Homeopathic HCG (HHCG) has become available. I have not personally tried this new homeopathic variety of HCG and there are no studies at this time showing whether it is as effective as using the natural HCG. Many dieters report success and lasting results in losing weight using the homeopathic versions of the HCG. If you are considering this alternative, always purchase homeopathic HCG from a reputable source. The homeopathic HCG is taken under the tongue like sublingual. Check with your homeopathic provider for more information.

Exercise caution when choosing this option simply because with the growing popularity and amazing results of the HCG Diet, homeopathic HCG suppliers are popping up all over the country and the internet. Due to the demand, a disreputable seller could literally sell you water and vitamins at significantly inflated prices and you may not achieve the lasting results and fat loss proven by using natural HCG or a quality homeopathic formulation.

The Four Phases of the HCG Diet

There are four steps or Phases of the HCG Diet. The first is "**Prep and Load**" (also known as Phase 1 or P1). The second is "**The HCG Phase**" (also known as Phase 2 or P2). The third is "**The Stabilization Phase**" (also known as Phase 3 or P3), and the fourth is "**The Maintenance Phase**" (also known as Phase 4 or P4).

Prep and Load

CLEANSING

Consider a period of detoxification and cleansing prior to beginning the HCG Diet. Performing colon cleanses, candida cleansing, and taking additional vitamin and mineral supplements to prepare the body for the diet can maximize weight loss and improve overall health. It is important to give your body high quality nutritious foods and supplements before and after the strict "HCG Phase" of the diet. Consider daily or occasional vegetable juicing during this time to provide extra healthy nutrients and energy. Many people have found that cleansing and detoxing prior to beginning the diet can really help maximize the benefit of the HCG Diet and assist with successful maintenance.

NUTRITIONAL LOADING

I highly recommend what I call "Nutritional Loading" before and after the "HCG Phase" of the diet which essentially means taking in quality supplements, a green drink, trace minerals, and eating quality healthy food including lots of fruits and vegetables. Taking supplements during the "HCG Phase" is not recommended by Dr. Simeons as it may slow or stall weight loss so it is important to build up the body systems before and after for optimal health.

HCG DIET *Tip* *Weigh yourself daily and keep a log of each day's progress.*

MENTAL PREPARATION

Prepare yourself mentally by committing to stick to the program. Clean out your cupboards and throw out or donate any food that could tempt you while on the diet. Take some before, during, and after pictures to help you stay motivated while on the diet as well as accurate measurements so you can track your progress along the way. Buy yourself an accurate digital food scale for preparing your meals and consider a new digital bathroom scale if you need one. A scale that measures your weight in .2 pound increments is best. During times of slower weight loss that .2 pound loss can help you stay motivated.

As you prepare for this diet, focus on your goals and list in your journal all the reasons you want to lose weight. Think about your health, your family, and all the ways losing the weight will change your life. Visualize yourself at your goal weight, buying new clothes, and feeling slim and healthy. Remember that you do not have to do this diet alone. Consider joining an HCG support group, and prepare your family and friends to support you in your weight loss journey.

2 DAYS OF FAT LOADING

For the first two days of the program, while taking the HCG, it is important to "Load" by eating high fat foods. This is an absolutely essential phase where you must eat a high calorie, high fat diet. Oils, cheeses, avocados, nuts, pastries, cream, fatty meats, and other rich foods are recommended for these two loading days.

It is very important not to skip this

phase. It is an absolutely necessary part of the diet. People who have skipped this step have reported being excessively hungry for the first week or two of the low calorie HCG Phase of the diet. It is not a particularly pleasant experience to eat the sheer volume of high fat food especially when you aren't used to it. Just do the best you can and don't hold back. Consider eating smaller amounts of high fat food every hour rather than large amounts of food at one sitting. Focusing on concentrated high fat food over carbohydrates will give you the best results. As a result of loading properly, you should experience little to no hunger when you transition into the 500 calorie diet of the HCG Phase of the diet.

The HCG Phase

During the "HCG Phase" (also known as Phase 2 or P2) of the diet, the dieter takes injections (once a day) of 125-200 iu doses of HCG daily or 150 iu SL HCG (twice a day) for a period of 23-43 days while observing a very specific, low fat, 500 calorie diet.

The food choices are very limited and specific and must be adhered to strictly in order for the diet to be successful. A list of allowed foods is provided for you in a later section of the book along with some per serving calorie counts to help keep your total calories for the day below 500.

During the "HCG Phase" it is important to avoid contact with all external fats such as creams and lotions. Dr. Simeons found that even trace amounts of externally applied oils could stall the weight loss process. Only powdered makeup, lipstick, and eye pencil may be used. In cases of severe dryness or cracking a small amount of mineral oil or aloe vera juice can be used on problem areas.

PLATEAUS

Plateaus are normal with this diet. Weight loss usually presents in a stair step fashion with a consistent large drop in weight followed by a slight plateau or slower losses for a few days. At least one significant plateau occurs in the second half of the protocol that often lasts 4-6 days. This is normal and will resolve itself in time so don't be alarmed when this occurs. If a plateau continues longer than 4 days an "Apple Day" can be considered.

THE APPLE DAY

Although most plateaus will resolve naturally on their own it can be very discouraging to experience several days without weight loss. An "Apple Day" can be used when a dieter reaches a plateau (no loss for a period of 4-5 days). The way to do an Apple day is to eat 6 apples over a 24 hour period and drink minimal water for the day — just enough to quench your thirst. This usually resolves the plateau and regular weight loss usually resumes the next morning.

The Stabilization Phase

The "Stabilization Phase" (also known as Phase 3 or P3) is a three week period following the "HCG Phase"

HCG DIET Tip

Take accurate measurements (chest, upper arms, waist, hips, buttocks, thighs, calves) before you start the program to help you track your progress. Take measurements again and record the results each week you are on the diet.

where you are allowed and encouraged to eat normal amounts of food and calories with the exception of starches and sugars. It is an important part of this diet protocol as it is the period where the weight and metabolism stabilize at a new, higher, metabolic set point.

For the first week or two on the "Stabilization Phase" you can expect wild fluctuations in your weight. This is normal and your weight will stabilize at some point during the three weeks. A glass of wine, beer, or other alcohol can be enjoyed on P3 without issue as well as a more varied and exciting diet. It is important for HCG dieters to weigh themselves daily on P3 and immediately do a Steak Day if a gain of over 2 pounds of your LIW/LSDW (Last Injection/Sublingial Dose Weight) occurs.

THE STEAK DAY

A steak day is done if a gain of over two pounds occurs after the morning weighing. To do a steak day, all food must be avoided throughout the day (water is fine) and then a large steak and either a raw apple or raw tomato must be consumed. The steak can be prepared with a variety of spices, but no salt. Doing a steak day will usually correct the weight gain by the following morning and you can resume your regular Phase 3 stabilizing diet. The steak day must be done the same day you notice the 2 pound gain. It is an important part of this phase of the diet and is critical to stabilizing the weight and resetting the metabolism.

The Maintenance Phase

The "Maintenance Phase" (also known as Phase 4 or P4) involves gradually introducing starches and carbohydrates back into your diet. This is the transition back to "real life" and normal eating patterns. Your weight should be monitored daily. I recommend a diet high in fiber and healthy grains, fruits, vegetables, and protein. I also recommend "Nutritional Loading" by taking healthy supplements and a green drink especially if you have multiple rounds to do and plan to go back on the "HCG Phase" to lose additional weight. I recommend doing your best to avoid processed food as much as possible and minimize sugar in your diet. Once you reach "The Maintenance Phase" you can pretty much eat anything you want as long as it is a healthy version of it.

HCG DIET *Tip*

It is helpful to keep a food diary to make sure you are consuming no more than 500 calories per day. A food diary can help you evaluate your weight loss and help you adjust your food choices if you plateau. Our bodies metabolize foods differently. Some people may have slower weight loss eating beef or oranges, for example, while others may not have a problem with these food items. A food diary can help you determine if a particular food is causing a problem with your weight loss.

Follow the HCG Diet strictly. The HCG Diet should be followed to the letter and without substitution. Only the specific fruits,

Guidelines for Success

vegetables, and allowed proteins should be used and in the correct amounts. A total of no more than 500 calories should be consumed to achieve the best results.

Don't Cheat

Cheating is not an option while using HCG during this diet. Eating a single peanut or anything not on the allowed list of food items can result in large and unpredictable gains even when the calorie count is low such as from a non-approved vegetable. If you do "cheat," recognize that you may lose about 3 days of weight loss and just get right back on the program.

Load Properly

Begin the diet by "loading" appropriately with rich and high fat foods for two days. Conclude the diet with 3 weeks of a starch and sugar free diet followed by a slow incorporation of carbohydrates and healthy starches. You may find that you are sensitive to certain high starch foods such as potatoes or that you need to minimize sugar in your diet for maintenance.

Weigh Yourself Every Day

It is important to weigh yourself every day during each phase of the diet and for life. This will keep you motivated while on the diet and allow you to monitor your weight and maintain it for life.

Avoid All Fats

Once the low calorie "HCG Phase" of the diet begins, all fats must be avoided. All meats must be trimmed and prepared without fat. All lotions, liquid makeup, and other externally applied products containing fats must be avoided.

No Substitutions

Do not substitute pork, other poultry, fatty fish, or heavily marbled beef for the lean protein choices recommended by Dr. Simeons. I personally stalled for 9 days during my first round on the "HCG Phase" because I ate very lean turkey breast. A chemical reaction is taking place in your body during this process and deviating from any of the recommendations made by Dr. Simeons can result in significant weight gain or water retention. Dr. Simeons' choices are the results of years of research and application with his patients in Rome. Don't try to do this by yourself, follow the plan and you will be successful.

Don't Mix Ingredients

Keep the ingredients in the recipes congruent. If you use chicken broth in a recipe, use it only with chicken and not beef or fish. If you utilize a marinade made with orange juice, eat the remainder of the fruit as your fruit choice for that meal.

Weigh Your Proteins

Weigh your proteins raw to exactly 100 grams and use a quality food scale to accurately measure your protein servings prior to cooking.

Drink Lots of Water

Make sure you are drinking enough water during the protocol. Your body is likely detoxifying during this process and you are metabolizing fat at such a rapid rate that you need to be able to flush out these toxins and waste materials. Drink plenty of water as well as the recommended teas to obtain the best results and maximize your success.

Summary of the HCG Diet

The HCG Diet can help you lose up to a pound a day on average. Prepare the body by cleansing and enjoying healthy food followed by 2 days of high fat "loading." Take your HCG in a dosage of 125-200 iu daily for a period of 23-43 days followed by a 3 week period of a normal calorie diet with the exception of starches and sugars to stabilize your weight and

metabolism. Finally, gradually introduce carbohydrates back into your diet and choose a healthy, whole food, high fiber diet for optimal maintenance of your new weight. Take breaks between rounds if you have a lot of weight to lose.

I recommend that anyone considering this protocol research the diet thoroughly, consult their physician, particularly if they have any major health concerns, and follow the plan correctly to get the best results and lasting weight loss.

HCG DIET Tip

Space out your meals throughout the day. This technique can help you avoid hunger and keep blood sugar levels constant. I recommend eating a fresh fruit for breakfast, a protein and vegetable for lunch, a protein and vegetable for dinner, and finally a fruit for an afternoon or evening snack. According to Dr. Simeons, you may skip all food until noon if you wish. Do what feels best for you but consider this as another option.

HCG Diet Foods

Protein Choices

You may have your choice of lean protein 100 grams, weighed raw. You should have two servings per day at different meals and all visible fat must be removed prior to cooking.

Chicken breast (skinless)
Beef
Veal
Fresh white fish
Lobster
Crab
Shrimp
100 grams low fat cottage cheese
1 whole egg plus 3 egg whites

Vegetable Choices

You may have one vegetable at each meal and two vegetable servings per day. Dr. Simeons cautioned against mixing vegetables on the HCG Diet. Different vegetable choices should be made for each meal when possible to maximize optimal nutrition and vitamins for the body. There are no specific limits on the amount of vegetables that are allowed per meal. Use your judgment. It is helpful to eat a little extra of a high fiber vegetable such as cabbage if occasional hunger occurs during the HCG Phase of the diet.

Spinach
Chicory
Chard
Beet-greens
Green salad
Celery
Tomatoes
Radishes
Onions
Cucumbers
Asparagus
Cabbage
Fennel

Fruits

You should have 2 servings of an allowed fruit. Be sure to eat your fruit servings at separate meals.

1 apple
1 orange
½ grapefruit
Handful of strawberries

Miscellaneous Allowed Foods

You may have unlimited or reasonable amounts of the following foods unless otherwise indicated.

Tea
Coffee
Mineral water
Juice of 1 lemon daily
Spices
Stevia
Two Melba toast, breadsticks or grissini (not at the same meal)
One tablespoon of milk allowed daily

Health Benefits of Spices

Cinnamon
Boosts brain function
Assists with blood sugar control
Antimicrobial properties
Antifungal properties
Anticlotting properties
Contains calcium, vitamins, and fiber
Aids in digestion

Curry and Turmeric
Anti-inflammatory
May decrease arthritis pain
May decrease risk of certain types of cancers
May protect against Alzheimer's disease
May decrease cholesterol
May boost brain function

Tarragon
Aids in digestion
May help with insomnia
Anti-inflammatory properties

Dill
Good source of calcium
Antibacterial properties
May have anti-carcinogenic properties

Cilantro (coriander seeds)
May help control blood sugar
May help cleanse heavy metals from the body
Antimicrobial properties
Rich in phyto-nutrients
May help decrease cholesterol
Aids in digestion

Cumin
Good source of iron
Anti-carcinogenic properties
Aids in digestion
Believed to be a blood purifier

Saffron
Aids in digestion
May help with depression

May have anti-carcinogenic properties
Rich in antioxidants

Black pepper
Aids in digestion
Rich in antioxidants
Antibacterial properties

Cayenne pepper
Anti-inflammatory
Pain relief
May help prevent ulcers
May assist with weight loss efforts by increasing metabolism
Improves circulation
Decreases mucous production

Basil
Good source of beta-carotene
Anti-inflammatory properties
Antibacterial properties
Rich in antioxidants

Ginger
Aids in digestion
Anti-inflammatory properties
Boosts the immune system
May protect against colon cancer

Mustard
Rich in phyto-nutrients
Anti-inflammatory properties
May improve cardiovascular health
Aids in digestion

Oregano
Antibacterial properties

HCG DIET *Tip*

Read Pounds and Inches *by Dr. A.T.W. Simeons and/or* The Weight Loss Cure They Don't Want You to Know About *by Kevin Trudeau. It is important to have a good understanding of the HCG Diet before you start.*

Rich in antioxidants
Aids in digestion
May assist with respiratory problems

Peppermint
Aids in digestion
Useful in aromatherapy
Makes a wonderful tea
Rich in phyto-nutrients

Rosemary
Anti-inflammatory properties
Rich in antioxidants
Anti-carcinogenic properties
Rich in vitamin E and minerals
A mild diuretic
May help to detoxify the liver
May improve brain function and
  memory

Sage
Anti-inflammatory
Antimicrobial properties
Rich in antioxidants
May improve brain function and
  memory

Thyme
Antibacterial properties
Rich in antioxidants
May benefit respiratory health
Improves circulation
Strengthens the immune system

Parsley
Improves circulation
Prevents bad breath
Rich in vitamins and minerals
Rich in antioxidants
Mild diuretic
May improve kidney function

Garlic
Antibacterial properties
Antiviral properties
Rich in antioxidants
May help decrease cholesterol

Onion
Antibacterial properties
May improve respiratory health
May help decrease cholesterol
May improve cardiovascular health

Lemon
Lemon oil may be helpful for dissolving
cellulite (phase 3 only)
Rich source of vitamin C
Boosts the immune system
Antibacterial properties
May be helpful for detoxifying the liver

Recommended Spices and Flavorings
Cayenne pepper
Mustard powder
Garlic powder
Onion powder
Black pepper
Rosemary
Thyme
Marjoram
Saffron
Curry
Oregano
Cumin
Himalayan pink salt
Alaua Hawaiian red and black salt
Stevia (comes in powdered or flavored
  liquid forms)

Organic seasoning blends (poultry, Italian, etc.)

Old Bay seasoning

Garam masala seasoning mix (Indian spice mixture)

Madagascar dry vanilla powder (use in moderation, contains trace amounts of maltodexterin)

Cocoa (use a defatted or low fat variety such as Wonderslim and in limited amounts)

Organic Worcestershire sauce (check the sugar content)

Bragg's liquid aminos

Hot sauce (made from cayenne pepper, avoid non-approved ingredients like sugar or jalapeno pepper) My favorite is Frank's red hot sauce

Bragg's organic raw apple cider vinegar

Liquid Smoke natural liquid hickory smoke flavoring

HCG DIET *Tip*

Enjoy Garlic, Fresh Herbs, and Dried Spices on the HCG Diet. I use small amounts of onion as a "spice" in my recipes. Feel free to experiment with unusual flavor combinations and spices. The variety will keep your meals delicious and interesting.

Calorie Counts for the Foods on the HCG Diet

I'm including approximate nutritional values and serving sizes for the foods allowed on the HCG Diet. The protein and fruit servings are very precise and exact but the vegetable servings are a recommended or approximate amount that you can use in the recipes. Dr. Simeons didn't put a limit on the vegetables so feel free to use more or less with the recipes; just make sure to keep your total calorie count for the day below 500.

Proteins
(values may vary slightly depending on cut or variety)

Chicken Breast: 100 grams contains 25 grams of protein, 2 grams of fat, and 135 calories

White Fish: 100 grams contains 20 grams of protein, 4 grams of fat, and 120 calories

Lean Beef: 100 grams contains 20 grams of protein, 5-10 grams fat (depending on the cut), and 140 calories

Shrimp/lobster/crab: 100 grams contains 20 grams of protein, 1.5 grams fat, and 100 calories

Fruit

1 medium apple: .5 grams protein, 0 fat, 90 calories

½ grapefruit: 1 gram protein, 0 fat, 50 calories

5 large strawberries: .5 grams protein, 0 fat, 30 calories

1 medium orange: 1 gram protein, 0 fat, 65 calories

Vegetables

Cabbage: 2 cups chopped = 1.5 grams protein, 0 grams fat, and 50 calories
Spinach: 2 cups chopped = 2 grams protein, 0 grams fat, and 25 calories
Tomatoes: 1 ½ cups chopped = 3 grams protein, 0 grams fat, 50 calories
Celery: 1 ½ cups chopped = 1 gram protein, 0 grams fat, 25 calories
8 medium radishes = 1 gram protein, 0 grams fat, 18 calories
1 medium cucumber = 2 grams protein, 0 grams fat, 45 calories
Lettuce/Mixed greens: 2 cups shredded = 0 protein, 0 fat, 10 calories
Asparagus: 1 ½ cups cooked = 5 grams protein, 0 fat, 60 calories
Fennel: 1 ½ cups cooked = 1 gram protein, 0 grams fat, 40 calories
Chicory: 1 cup raw = 1 gram protein, 0 grams fat, 15 calories
Beet Greens: 1 ½ cups cooked = 1 gram protein, 0 grams fat, 15 calories
Chard: 1 ½ cups cooked = 1 gram protein, 0 grams fat, 55 calories

Miscellaneous Ingredients

Dried spices: 0 protein, 0 fat, less than 10 calories
Fresh ginger: 1 tablespoon = 0 protein, 0 fat, less than 5 calories
1 clove garlic = 0 protein, 0 fat, less than 5 calories
Minced onion: 1 tablespoon = 0 protein, 0 fat, less than 5 calories
Bragg's liquid aminos: 1 teaspoon = .5 grams protein, 0 fat, 0 calories
Apple cider vinegar: 1 tablespoon = 0 protein, 0 fat, 0 calories
Cayenne pepper sauce: 1 teaspoon. = 0 protein, 0 fat, 0 calories
Fat free milk: 1 tablespoon = .2 grams protein, 0 fat, less than 5 calories
1 Melba toast = .5 grams protein, 0 fat, 18 calories
Lemon juice: 1 ounce = 0 protein, 0 fat, 8 calories
Chicken broth: 1 cup = 1.5 grams protein, 0-1 grams fat, 15 calories
Beef broth: 1 cup = 1 gram protein, 0-1 grams fat, 10 calories
Stevia: 0 protein, 0 fat, 0 calories

HCG DIET Tip *Choose Organic Foods. Organic foods are grown/raised without hormones, pesticides, and other unhealthy chemicals. Choosing organic is optional. You will still lose weight if you don't choose to eat organic, but I encourage you to consider making this change for your health.*

Sweet Japanese Cucumber Salad

Ingredients
1 cucumber, sliced/ diced
2 tablespoons apple cider vinegar
1 tablespoon fresh lemon juice
1 teaspoon Bragg's liquid aminos
1 teaspoon finely minced onion
Cayenne pepper to taste
Stevia to taste

Makes 1 serving
(1 vegetable)

2 grams protein

0 fat

49 calories

▶ Mix ingredients together, marinate for 15 minutes or more, and
  serve chilled.

Variations: Marinate cucumbers in **Sweet Wasabi Marinade.**

Cold Curried Chicken Salad

Ingredients
100 grams chicken, diced
1 apple, diced
1 ½ cups celery, diced (optional)
¼ cup water
2 tablespoons lemon juice
1 tablespoon finely minced onion
1 clove of garlic, crushed and minced
¼ teaspoon curry powder or to taste
Dash of garlic powder
Dash of onion powder
Dash of cayenne pepper
Dash of cinnamon
Dash of turmeric
Stevia to taste

Makes 1 serving
(1 protein, 1 vegetable,
1 fruit)

27 grams protein

3 fat

260 calories

▶ In small saucepan lightly sauté chicken in lemon juice until lightly
  brown. Add ¼ cup water and spices. Stir well and simmer over low heat
    until liquid reduces to form a sauce and chicken is cooked well. Add
water as needed to create the consistency you want. Chill, add chopped
apple and celery or omit the celery and serve over a green salad.

H C G
D I E T
Tip

*Dilute the strong
flavor of apple
cider vinegar by
mixing it with a
little Stevia or a
few teaspoons of
water or broth.*

Lobster Salad

Ingredients
100 grams lobster tail, diced
1 ½ cups celery, sliced, steamed fennel bulb, or tomatoes (optional)
1 tablespoon lemon juice
1 teaspoon apple cider vinegar
Pinch of chopped green onion
Pinch of tarragon
Salt and black pepper to taste
Stevia to taste

▸ Mix lobster, liquid ingredients and spices together and serve over a salad, arugula greens, or with another vegetable.

Makes 1 serving
(1 protein, 1 vegetable)

22 grams protein

2 fat

140 calories

PHASE 3
MODIFICATIONS:
Stir in 1-2 tablespoons mayonnaise or sour cream. You can also add any kind of fresh fruit like grapes, diced apple, or top with Stevia caramelized pear slices. Add a small amount of chopped walnuts, almonds, or pine nuts for added crunch.

Spicy Crab Salad

Ingredients
100 grams crab
1 cup celery, diced (optional)
1 tablespoon lemon juice
2 teaspoons apple cider vinegar
1 teaspoon Bragg's liquid aminos
1 tablespoon finely minced red onion
Dash of garlic powder
Dash of onion powder
Cayenne pepper to taste
Salt and black pepper to taste
You may substitute 1 teaspoon of Old Bay seasoning for the powdered ingredients.

▸ Steam the crab and chop into medium chunks. Toss with onions, spices, and liquid ingredients. Marinate for 15 minutes or more and serve over mixed green salad or add diced celery.

Makes 1 serving
(1 protein, 1 vegetable)

22 grams protein

2 fat

120 calories

Shrimp Cocktail

Ingredients
100 grams raw shrimp (approximately 10-12 medium shrimp), steamed

Cocktail sauce
2 ounces tomato paste
2 tablespoons lemon juice
1 tablespoon apple cider vinegar
1 teaspoon hot sauce
1/8 teaspoon of horseradish or to taste
Dash of mustard powder
Stevia to taste
Salt and pepper to taste
Water as needed for desired consistency

Makes 1 serving (1 protein, 1 vegetable)
24 grams protein
2 fat
150 calories

▸ Mix tomato paste, vinegar, horseradish, lemon juice and spices together and allow spices to marinate and dipping sauce to chill. Add water as needed to create desired consistency. Steam the shrimp until pink and well cooked. Chill shrimp for 30 minutes in the refrigerator and serve with cocktail dipping sauce.

Chilled Garlic Refrigerator Pickles

Ingredients
One medium cucumber, sliced into rounds
4 cloves of garlic, thinly sliced
¼- ½ cup apple cider vinegar
3 tablespoons lemon juice
Salt

Makes 1-2 servings (1 vegetable)
2 grams protein
0 fat
50 calories

▸ Mix liquid ingredients together. Salt cucumber slices well. Pack cucumber slices tightly into a small glass canning jar layering garlic slices in between layers. Pour apple cider vinegar and lemon juice into container until liquid covers the slices. Refrigerate overnight. Pickles can be refrigerated for up to 4 days. Or marinate cucumber slices in salt, vinegar and garlic, then use a pickle press or weighted plate to press out excess liquid.

Orange Cabbage Salad with Chicken

Ingredients
100 grams of chicken
2 cups chopped, any kind of cabbage
One orange (3 tablespoons of juice and remaining orange sliced or in segments)
1 tablespoon apple cider vinegar
2 tablespoons lemon juice
1 tablespoon Bragg's liquid aminos
Pinch of fresh or powdered ginger
Dash of cayenne (optional)
Stevia to taste (optional)
Salt and fresh black pepper to taste

Makes 1 serving
(1 protein, 1 vegetable, 1 fruit)

28.5 grams protein

3 fat

255 calories

PHASE 3 MODIFICATIONS: Add a drizzle of olive or sesame oil, top with sliced almonds or sesame seeds.

▶ Marinate strips or chunks of chicken in apple cider vinegar, lemon juice and spices. Cook thoroughly, browning slightly. Prepare dressing with 3 tablespoons of orange juice, Bragg's, Stevia, black pepper, salt, and cayenne. You may add extra apple cider vinegar, if desired. Shred cabbage into coleslaw consistency and toss lightly with dressing. Allow to marinate for at least 20 minutes or overnight. Top with chicken and orange slices.

Cold Asparagus Salad

Ingredients
1 ½ cups asparagus spears
3 tablespoons lemon juice
Fresh mint leaves or parsley, chopped
2 tablespoons caper juice
1 tablespoon finely minced red onion
Salt and pepper to taste

Makes 1 serving
(1 vegetable)

5 grams protein

0 fat

65 calories

PHASE 3 MODIFICATIONS: Add olive oil or drizzle with melted butter.

▶ Lightly steam the asparagus until tender. Marinate in juices and spices for at least 30 minutes and enjoy. Variations: Toss with the marinade of your choice for flavor variety.

Red Cabbage Salad

Ingredients
2 cups red cabbage, chopped
¼ cup apple cider vinegar
2 tablespoons Bragg's liquid aminos
3 tablespoons lemon juice
¼ teaspoon onion powder
¼ teaspoon garlic powder
1 clove finely minced garlic
1 tablespoon finely minced onion
Cayenne pepper to taste
Stevia to taste
Salt and black pepper to taste

Makes 1-2 servings
(1 vegetable)

2 grams protein

0 fat

60 calories

PHASE 3
MODIFICATIONS: Add olive oil or flax seed oil. Toss with crumbled bacon or Gorgonzola cheese.

> Combine spices with liquid ingredients. Coat cabbage thoroughly with dressing and marinate for 1-2 hours or overnight to blend flavors.

Cucumber Orange Salad

Ingredients
1 cucumber, sliced
Orange slices (1 orange)
Orange juice from 3 segments
1 tablespoon lemon juice
1 teaspoon apple cider vinegar (try **Tarragon and Garlic Infusion**)
1 teaspoon fresh tarragon, minced
1 tablespoon red onion, minced
Salt and pepper to taste
Stevia to taste
Fresh mint leaves, chopped (optional)

Makes one serving
(1 vegetable, 1 fruit)

3 grams protein

0 fat

115 calories

PHASE 3
MODIFICATIONS:
Drizzle with hazelnut oil, top with toasted pine nuts.

> Combine apple cider vinegar, Stevia , onion, and spices. Mix well. Add cucumber and orange slices, tarragon, salt, and pepper to taste. Marinate for 30 minutes. Garnish with fresh mint leaves.

Coleslaw/Apple Slaw

Ingredients
2 cups cabbage, chopped
1 apple, diced (optional)
2 tablespoons lemon juice
1 tablespoon apple cider vinegar
¼ teaspoon garlic powder
Dash of mustard powder
Dash of cinnamon (optional)
Salt and pepper to taste
Stevia to taste

Makes 1-2 servings
(1 vegetable coleslaw)
(1 vegetable, 1 fruit apple slaw)

2 grams protein

0 fat

145 calories

PHASE 3
MODIFICATIONS: Add mayonnaise or Greek yogurt for a creamier texture.

> Slice cabbage in very thin strips. Toss with lemon juice and spices. Allow to marinate for 30 minutes or overnight. Add apples and 1/8 teaspoon cinnamon to make an apple slaw.

Citrus and Fennel Salad

Ingredients
½ grapefruit, cut into medium chunks or 1 orange in segments
Fennel bulb, steamed
2 tablespoons lemon juice
Mint or cilantro, chopped
Stevia to taste

Makes 1 serving
(1 vegetable, 1 fruit)

2 grams protein

0 fat

90 calories

PHASE 3
MODIFICATIONS: Drizzle with olive oil and top with pine nuts.

> Slice fennel bulb and cut citrus into chunks. Combine ingredients in a bowl. Mix well and chill.

Spicy Thai Cucumber Salad

Ingredients
1 whole cucumber, cut julienne style
1 tablespoon Bragg's liquid aminos
2 tablespoons lemon juice
2 tablespoons vegetable broth (optional)
1 tablespoon green onion, chopped
1 clove of garlic, crushed and minced
1 basil leaf, rolled and sliced
1 teaspoon cilantro leaves, chopped
1/8 teaspoon red chili flakes
Salt and pepper to taste
Stevia to taste

Makes 1-2 servings
(1 vegetable)

2 grams protein

1 gram fat

50 calories

PHASE 3
MODIFICATIONS: Add
a little sesame oil or
chili oil. Add chopped
bell pepper or other
vegetables. Top with a
tablespoon of crushed
peanuts.

Chop up cucumber in julienne strips. Mix liquid ingredients with the garlic, onion, fresh herbs, and chili flakes. Mix in cucumbers and coat thoroughly with spice mixture. Allow to marinate for 10 minutes or overnight.

Crunchy Sweet Apple Chicken Salad

Ingredients
100 grams chicken, cooked and diced
1 apple, diced
1 ½ cups celery, diced
3 tablespoons lemon juice
1/8 teaspoon cinnamon
Dash of nutmeg
Dash of cardamom
Dash of salt
Stevia to taste
Wedge of lemon

Makes 1 serving
(1 protein, 1 vegetable,
1 fruit)

27 grams protein,

2 grams fat

255 calories

PHASE 3
MODIFICATIONS:
Add chopped walnuts
or raw almonds. Mix
in low sugar Greek
yogurt or 1 tablespoon
of mayonnaise for a
creamier texture.

Mix ingredients together. Sprinkle with Stevia and cinnamon. Chill for 20 minutes. Serve with a wedge of lemon and enjoy.

Curried Celery Salad

Ingredients
1 ½ cups celery, diced
1 tablespoon Bragg's liquid aminos
3 tablespoons lemon juice
1 tablespoon apple cider vinegar
1 tablespoon green onions, chopped
Curry to taste
Stevia to taste

Makes 1 serving
(1 vegetable)

1 gram protein

0 fat

27 calories

▶ Add spices to liquid ingredients and mix thoroughly. Coat celery
thoroughly and allow flavors to marinate for 20-30 minutes and serve.

Ceviche

Ingredients
100 grams white fish or shrimp, chilled and cooked
3 tablespoons lemon or lime juice
1 ½ cups tomatoes, diced
1 tablespoon onion, chopped
1 clove garlic, crushed and minced
Fresh cilantro, chopped
Dash hot sauce
Salt and pepper to taste

Makes 1 serving
(1 protein, 1 vegetable)

23 grams protein

4 grams fat

175 calories

PHASE 3
MODIFICATIONS:
Add diced jalapeno,
add additional types
of seafood. Serve over
cream cheese for a
vegetable dip. For a
sweeter ceviche, try
adding a little fresh fruit.

▶ Steam the shrimp or fish. Add lemon, onion, garlic, and chopped
cilantro. Stir in diced tomatoes and hot sauce. Chill and marinate the
ingredients in the refrigerator. Traditionally, ceviche is not cooked. The
citric acids "cook" the fish. This is an alternative to cooking the shrimp or
fish.

Cold Fennel Salad

Ingredients
1 ½ cups fennel bulb, steamed and diced
2 tablespoons lemon juice
1 teaspoon apple cider vinegar (optional)
1 teaspoon red onion, minced
Dash of turmeric
Salt and pepper to taste
Stevia to taste
Fresh mint leaves, chopped (optional)

Makes 1 serving
(1 serving vegetable)

1 gram protein

0 fat

45 calories

Steam fennel until bulb is tender. Marinate fennel in vinegar and spices or any marinade and chill until ready to serve. Serve with appropriate fruit or lemon juice. Add salt and pepper to taste. Works well with chopped apple or slices of orange. (Only use the orange if you marinated with orange juice, remember not to mix fruits.)

Cucumber and Strawberry Salad

Ingredients
1 whole cucumber
3 large strawberries, sliced
1 serving **Strawberry Vinaigrette**
Fresh ground white pepper
Stevia to taste

Makes 1-2 servings
(1 vegetable, 1 fruit)

2 grams protein

0 fat

78 calories

Slice strawberries and cucumber. Toss dressing, Stevia and pepper with strawberries to taste. Allow to marinate for at least 10 minutes.

HCG
DIET
Tip   *Prepare a side or entree salad in advance for an "on the go" meal.*

Chinese Chicken Salad

Ingredients
100 grams chicken breast
2 cups cabbage, chopped
1 tablespoon Bragg's liquid aminos
1 tablespoon apple cider vinegar
1 tablespoon green onion, minced
1 clove of garlic, crushed and minced
1 teaspoon fresh ginger, grated (substitute a dash of powdered ginger)
Pinch of red pepper flakes
Stevia to taste
Salt and pepper to taste

Makes 1 serving
(1 protein, 1 vegetable)
27 grams protein
2 grams fat
190 calories

PHASE 3
MODIFICATIONS: Drizzle with sesame oil. Add additional vegetables such as bell pepper and mushrooms. Sprinkle with toasted almonds or sesame seeds.

▸ Brown the chicken with lemon juice, 1 tablespoon Bragg's, garlic, and onion. Slice cabbage into fine strips. Steam lightly until cooked. Drain off excess liquid. Add chicken, ginger, salt and pepper, and chill. Sprinkle with additional Bragg's.

Asparagus and Apple Salad

Ingredients
1 ½ cups of asparagus, chopped
1 apple, diced
4 tablespoons lemon juice and water, as needed
¼ teaspoon garam masala or cinnamon
1 tablespoon onion, finely minced
Salt and pepper to taste
Stevia to taste

Makes 1 serving
(1 vegetable, 1 fruit)
6 grams protein
0 fat
150 calories

▸ Marinate asparagus in vinaigrette for 10 minutes or so. Lightly sauté asparagus in lemon juice until just lightly cooked. Toss with finely chopped onion, apple, and spices. Add salt, pepper, and Stevia to taste. Chill in refrigerator for 10 minutes and serve as a salad or hot as a side dish.

Arugula Salad with Chicken and Fruit

Ingredients
100 grams of chicken
2 cups of arugula greens
Your choice of apple, orange, strawberry or grapefruit slices
Dressing made from your choice of compatible fruit
1 tablespoon red onion, chopped
Salt and pepper to taste

Makes 1 serving
(1 protein, 1 vegetable,
1 fruit)

25 grams protein

2 fat

185-245 calories
(depending on the fruit
you use)

▸ Cook chicken with a little lemon juice and water until slightly browned. Prepare and wash arugula. Lay chicken slices on top of arugula salad and top with fruit and a dressing made from your fruit of choice.

Examples: **Strawberry Vinaigrette, Grapefruit Vinaigrette, Spicy Orange Dressing**, etc. See recipes for Dressings, Sauces, and Marinades.

Horseradish Slaw

Ingredients
2 cups cabbage, finely chopped
¼ cup apple cider vinegar
3 tablespoons broth (beef, vegetable, or chicken)
1 tablespoon Bragg's liquid aminos
1 tablespoon lemon juice
1 tablespoon red onion, minced
¼ teaspoon horseradish or to taste
Pinch of celery seeds
Salt and black pepper to taste

Makes 1-2 servings
(1 vegetable)

2 grams protein

.5 gram fat

60 calories

PHASE 3
MODIFICATIONS: Add
¼ cup mayonnaise. Omit
the lemon juice and
vinegar.

▸ Chop up cabbage finely. Discard any tough parts of the cabbage. In a small bowl combine the liquid ingredients, horseradish, and spices.
Toss dressing mixture with cabbage. Allow to marinate for at least an hour or overnight.

Melba Toast with Strawberry Jam

Ingredients
1 Melba toast
5 large strawberries
Stevia to taste

Makes 1 serving
(1 Melba toast, 1 fruit)

1 gram protein

0 fat

45 calories

▸ Puree fresh strawberries with Stevia and serve on top of Melba toast or sprinkle crushed Melba toast over strawberry puree for a wonderful crunchy texture.

Variations: add a little vanilla powder or cinnamon to the crushed Melba toast for additional flavor.

Melba Croutons

Cinnamon
Ingredients
1 serving Melba toast
Lemon juice
Pinch of cinnamon
Nutmeg
Powdered Stevia

Makes 1 serving
(1 Melba toast)

.5 grams protein

0 fat

22 calories

Garlic
Ingredients
1 serving Melba toast
Lemon juice
Pinch of garlic powder
Pinch of onion powder
Paprika
Salt and pepper to taste

▸ Sprinkle the Melba toast with lemon juice and spices and bake for 5 minutes in a 350 degree oven or dust dry with your choice of spices.

HCG DIET Tip

Keep extra allowed vegetable servings on hand if you get hungry. Dr. Simeons did not put a specific limit on vegetables. The standard amounts I've included in the recipes are meant to be a guideline. You may add additional vegetables to your meals up to a total of 500 calories per day.

Melba Toast with Spicy Cucumber

Ingredients
1 Melba toast
2-3 slices of cucumber (serve with the rest of the cucumber on the side)
1 tablespoon apple cider vinegar
Pinch of red onion, minced
Pinch of onion and garlic powder to taste
Dash of cayenne or chili pepper
Salt and pepper to taste

Makes 1 serving
(1 Melba toast,
1 vegetable)

2.5 grams protein

0 fat

62 calories

> Combine spices with apple cider vinegar. Marinate cucumber slices in spice mixture. Top Melba toast with cucumber and sprinkle with onion. Save additional cucumber for an additional snack. Variations: sprinkle the crumbs on top of a cucumber salad.

Chicken Salad with Celery Sticks

Makes 1 serving
(1 protein, 1 vegetable)

26 grams protein

2 fat

165 calories

Ingredients
100 grams of chicken
1 ½ cups celery, chopped
1 tablespoon Bragg's liquid aminos
1 tablespoon lemon juice
1 teaspoon apple cider vinegar
¼ teaspoon organic poultry seasoning
1 tablespoon onion, minced
Salt and pepper to taste

> Cook chicken in a little water or chicken broth. Finely chop all ingredients. Mix with spices and additional liquid ingredients. Serve with celery sticks or mix in diced celery and your choice of dressing or dipping sauce.

Note: When using a marinade that uses part of a fruit or vegetable in it, make sure to eat the remainder of the fruit or vegetable serving as part of that meal to ensure that you get a complete serving.

Strawberry Vinaigrette (enjoy with arugula salad)

Ingredients
2 Strawberries
1 tablespoon apple cider vinegar
1 tablespoon lemon juice
Stevia to taste
Dash of salt
Dash of cayenne (optional)
Fresh black pepper, ground to taste
Stevia to taste

Makes 1 serving (1 fruit)
0 grams protein
0 fat
10 calories

▶ Combine all ingredients in food processor. Puree until smooth. Pour over fresh arugula or green salad. Garnish with sliced strawberries and freshly ground black pepper. Variations: use as a marinade or sauce for chicken.

Savory Dill Dressing/Marinade

Ingredients
Fresh dill, minced
2 tablespoons lemon juice
2 tablespoons apple cider vinegar
2 tablespoon chicken or vegetable broth
½ teaspoon Old Bay seasoning mix
Salt and pepper to taste

Makes 1 serving
0 grams protein
0 fat
5 calories

▶ Combine ingredients, allow the flavors to marinate for 30 minutes or more and serve as a marinade for fish or a dressing for vegetables or salad. For use as a marinade, double or triple the recipe as needed.

Orange Tarragon Marinade

Ingredients
¼ cup chicken or vegetable broth
2 tablespoons apple cider vinegar
½ orange, juiced
1 clove of garlic, crushed and minced
1 teaspoon fresh tarragon, chopped
¼ teaspoon onion powder
Salt and pepper to taste

Makes 1 serving (1 fruit)
1 gram protein
.5 gram fat
35 calories

▶ Combine liquid ingredients with spices and cook on low heat for 3
minutes. Remove from heat and cool. Marinate chicken or fish for
20 minutes or more. Cook your protein (chicken, seafood, or beef) in
remaining marinade. Deglaze the pan periodically with a little water. Save
the sauce and add apple cider vinegar to make additional dressing for a
salad. Serve over a mixed green salad or with other vegetable.

Tarragon Vinegar Infusion

Ingredients
¼ cup apple cider vinegar
Fresh tarragon

Makes multiple servings
0 protein
0 fat
0 calories

▶ Combine vinegar with fresh tarragon in a lidded jar. Crush or roll the
tarragon slightly to release the flavor. Allow flavors to infuse into the
vinegar overnight or up to a week. Use as a marinade for fish or as the
base for a dressing. Add salt and pepper to taste.

Citrus Ginger Dressing/Marinade

Ingredients
1 tablespoon lemon juice
2 tablespoons orange juice
1 teaspoon apple cider vinegar
1 tablespoon Bragg's liquid aminos
Ginger, fresh or ground to taste
Salt and fresh black pepper to taste
Stevia to taste

Makes 1-2 serving (1 fruit) Serve with additional orange slices to complete a fruit serving

.5 grams protein

0 fat

less than 5 calories

> Combine spices with liquid ingredients. Enjoy over salad or double the recipe for use as a marinade. Warm slightly to enhance the flavors.

Teriyaki Sauce

Ingredients
½ cup beef or chicken broth (depending on your protein choice)
3 tablespoons Bragg's liquid aminos
2 tablespoons apple cider vinegar
Orange juice (juice from 4 segments)
2 tablespoons lemon juice
1 tablespoon onion, finely minced
1 teaspoon garlic powder
1 teaspoon onion powder
½ teaspoon powdered ginger or fresh ginger, grated
2 cloves garlic, finely minced
Lemon and/or orange zest to taste
Stevia to taste

Makes 1-2 servings (1 fruit)

.5 grams protein

.5 fat

20 calories

> Combine all ingredients in a small saucepan and bring to a boil. Reduce heat and simmer for 20 minutes or until liquid is reduced.

The longer you simmer, the richer the flavors. As the liquid reduces, deglaze the pan with a little water or broth to intensify the flavors. Enjoy as a glaze or sauce with chicken or beef.

Horseradish Marinade/Dipping Sauce

Ingredients
¼ cup beef broth
1 teaspoon of horseradish or to taste
½ teaspoon garlic powder
¼ teaspoon paprika

Makes 1-2 servings
.5 gram protein
0 fat
5 calories

▶ Whisk the ingredients together and heat the sauce in a small saucepan. Pour into dipping bowl or use as a sauce or marinade and enjoy with beef dishes.

Ketchup

Ingredients
2 tablespoons tomato paste
3 tablespoons apple cider vinegar
1 tablespoon lemon juice
¼ teaspoon celery salt
½ teaspoon paprika
¼ teaspoon mustard powder
Pinch of nutmeg and clove
Pinch of black pepper
¼ teaspoon onion powder
¼ teaspoon garlic powder
Stevia to taste

Makes 2 servings
(1 vegetable)
.5 gram protein
0 fat
20 calories per serving

▶ Dissolve spices in vinegar and lemon juice. Add tomato paste and mix thoroughly. Add additional lemon juice, vinegar or a little water until desired consistency is reached.

HCG DIET *Tip* *Enjoy Bragg's Liquid Amino's. A product I enjoy and use in many of my recipes is Bragg's liquid aminos. I use the liquid aminos as a replacement for traditional soy sauce in many of my recipes. Unlike regular soy sauce, it doesn't appear to affect weight loss with the HCG Diet.*

Marinara Sauce

Ingredients

1 ½ cups tomatoes, chopped or more if you wish to increase the recipe
1 cup chicken or vegetable broth
1 6 ounce can tomato paste
1 tablespoon dried basil or fresh basil, rolled and chopped to taste
2 tablespoons onion, minced
2 cloves of garlic, crushed and minced
1 teaspoon dried oregano
Cayenne pepper to taste
Pinch of marjoram
Salt and pepper to taste

Makes 3 servings
(1 vegetable)

2 grams protein

1 fat

71 calories per serving

▸ Chop tomatoes or puree in a food processor for a smoother texture, add spices and heat in a saucepan. Allow to slow cook for 30 minutes to an hour. Allow the liquid to reduce or add additional water to achieve desired consistency.

Tomato Picante Dressing

Ingredients

1 ½ cups tomatos, chopped
3 ounces tomato paste
1 clove garlic, crushed and chopped
1 teaspoon mustard powder
2 tablespoons lemon juice
½ teaspoon ground cumin
½ teaspoon chili powder
Pinch cayenne pepper
Salt and black pepper to taste
Apple cider vinegar to taste

Makes 4 servings
(1 vegetable)

1 gram protein

0 fat

32 calories per serving

▸ Put tomato and garlic into food processor and puree. Add mustard, lemon juice, cumin, chili powder, cayenne, salt, and tomato sauce. Blend until smooth. Transfer to a jar and refrigerate. Stir before using.

Homemade Mustard

Ingredients
2 tablespoons ground mustard powder
1 tablespoon garlic powder
1 tablespoon onion powder
½ teaspoon ginger, ground
½ teaspoon horseradish, grated (optional)
½ cup apple cider vinegar
¼ cup water
1 tablespoon lemon juice
Stevia to taste

Makes 1-2 servings
0 protein
0 fat
10 calories

> Mix ingredients together thoroughly, heat in a saucepan for 2-3 minutes. Pack warm mustard into a jar and top with lemon juice. Mustard will last up to two weeks in the refrigerator. Add water as needed for consistency.

Grapefruit Vinaigrette

Ingredients
Juice of 3 segments of grapefruit
1 tablespoon lemon juice
1 teaspoon apple cider vinegar (optional)
Stevia to taste

Makes 1-2 servings
(1 fruit when you eat the remainder with your meal)
.5 gram protein
0 fat
25 calories

> Combine juices and vinegar. Add Stevia to taste. Pour over mixed green salad and top with remaining grapefruit segments. Use as a marinade for fish, shrimp or chicken. Add salt and fresh ground pepper.

Tomato Basil Vinaigrette

Ingredients

3 tablespoons tomato paste
3 tablespoons apple cider vinegar
2 tablespoons lemon juice
¼ cup water, chicken or vegetable broth
1 tablespoon onion, minced
½ teaspoon garlic powder
½ teaspoon onion powder
1 teaspoon dried basil or basil leaves, fresh rolled and sliced to taste
1/8 teaspoon oregano
Cayenne pepper to taste
Stevia to taste

Makes 2-3 servings
(1 vegetable)
.5 grams protein
0 fat
20 calories per serving

> Combine ingredients in a small saucepan and heat slightly to a boil. Adjust liquid to desired consistency by adding a little more water or broth. Remove from heat and chill. Enjoy over salad with fresh ground black pepper.

Italian Vinaigrette

Ingredients

½ cup chicken or vegetable broth
2 tablespoons apple cider vinegar
2 tablespoons lemon juice
1 teaspoon organic Italian herb spice blend
2 tablespoons onion, finely minced
½ teaspoon garlic powder
½ teaspoon onion powder

Makes 2 or more servings
0 protein
0 fat
5 calories per serving

PHASE 3
MODIFICATIONS:
Add olive oil or omit
the lemon juice and
stir in sour cream or
mayonnaise to make
creamy Italian dressing.

> Combine ingredients in small saucepan. Simmer on low heat for 5 minutes to combine flavors. Remove from heat, chill, and serve as a dressing or use as a marinade.

Hot Cajun Dressing/Dipping Sauce

Ingredients
3 tablespoons apple cider vinegar
1 tablespoon lemon juice
Dash of garlic powder
Dash of onion powder
Cayenne pepper to taste
Salt and black pepper to taste
¼ teaspoon Old Bay seasoning mix (optional)
Stevia (optional)

Makes 1-2 servings
0 protein
0 fat
5 calories

> Combine ingredients in small bowl and pour over salad. You can also serve this as a dipping sauce or marinade for vegetables or fish.

Salsa

Ingredients
1 ½ cups fresh tomatoes, chopped
3 tablespoons lemon juice
1 tablespoon apple cider vinegar (optional)
2 cloves garlic, crushed and minced
2 tablespoons onion, finely chopped
¼ teaspoon chili powder
¼ teaspoon fresh or dried oregano
Cayenne pepper to taste
Fresh cilantro, chopped
Salt and pepper to taste

Makes 2 servings
(1 vegetable)
1 gram protein
0 fat
26 calories per serving

PHASE 3
MODIFICATIONS: Add chopped jalapeno or chipotle peppers. Mix with avocado to make guacamole. Serve salsa over a block of cream cheese as a dip for vegetables.

> Puree ingredients in food processor for smooth salsa or chop ingredients by hand for chunkier salsa. Add spices and chill in the refrigerator for 10 minutes or more to allow flavors to blend.

Barbecue Sauce

Ingredients
3 ounces tomato paste
¼ cup apple cider vinegar
3 tablespoons lemon juice
1 tablespoon hot sauce
1 tablespoon onion, minced
3 cloves garlic, crushed and minced
¼ teaspoon chili powder
Liquid smoke hickory flavoring to taste
½ teaspoon Worcestershire sauce
½ teaspoon garlic powder
½ teaspoon onion powder
1 teaspoon parsley, chopped
Stevia to taste (try a touch of dark chocolate liquid Stevia for added flavor)
Cayenne pepper to taste
Salt and pepper to taste
Water as needed to achieve desired consistency

Makes 2 servings
(1 vegetable)

.5 gram protein

0 fat

38 calories per serving

▶ In a small saucepan, combine all ingredients. Mix well and bring to
a boil. Reduce heat and simmer for at least 5 minutes adding a little
water to achieve desired consistency and to make sure it doesn't burn.
Use as a barbecue sauce for chicken or beef.

Marinated Apple Relish

Ingredients
1 apple, finely minced
1 stalk of celery, minced (optional)
2 tablespoons apple cider vinegar
2 tablespoons lemon juice
1 teaspoon red onion, minced
Dash of Worcestershire sauce
Salt and pepper to taste
Stevia to taste

Makes 1 serving
(1 fruit, 1 vegetable)

1 gram protein

0 fat

120 calories

▶ Mix apples and celery together. Dissolve spices into liquid ingredients
and pour over the apple mixture. Mix well and allow ingredients to
marinate for 30 minutes or longer to allow flavors to blend.

Sweet Wasabi Dipping Sauce/Marinade

Ingredients
¼ teaspoon wasabi powder or to taste (Japanese horseradish)
2 or more tablespoons Bragg's liquid aminos
1 tablespoon lemon juice
 Stevia to taste

> Mix wasabi into Bragg's and add lemon juice and Stevia to taste.

Makes 1 serving
0 protein
0 fat
5 calories

Sweet Orange Dressing/Marinade

Ingredients
Juice of 3 orange segments
2 tablespoons lemon juice
1 teaspoon apple cider vinegar (optional)
¼ teaspoon ginger powder
Pinch of turmeric
Pinch of orange zest
Stevia to taste

> Dissolve spices and Stevia in juice mixture. Heat the dressing slightly
> in a saucepan, then chill until ready to use. You may double the recipe
> for a marinade. Serve with remaining orange slices.

Makes 1 serving (1 fruit)
.5 grams protein
0 fat
20 calories

French Dressing

Ingredients
¼ cup beef broth
2 tablespoons apple cider vinegar
2 tablespoons lemon juice
1 clove garlic, crushed and minced
¼ teaspoon horseradish or to taste
½ teaspoon paprika
1/8 teaspoon mustard powder
Cayenne pepper to taste
Stevia to taste

> Dissolve spices in broth, vinegar and lemon juice. Mix well and heat
> slightly in small saucepan. Chill and serve over mixed greens or
> vegetables.

Makes 2 servings
0 protein
0 fat
10 calories

Sweet and Spicy Mustard Dressing

Ingredients
2 tablespoons **Homemade Mustard** recipe
2 tablespoons apple cider vinegar
2 tablespoons lemon juice
1 tablespoon Bragg's liquid aminos
Pinch of turmeric
1 clove garlic, finely minced
1 tablespoon onion, minced
Stevia to taste
Water to desired consistency

Makes 1-2 servings	
0 protein	
0 fat	
5 calories per serving	

Dissolve spices in liquid ingredients. Mix thoroughly and heat slightly in a saucepan. Add a little water or extra vinegar to create desired consistency.

Lemon Pepper Dressing/Marinade

Ingredients
4 tablespoons lemon juice
3 tablespoons chicken or vegetable broth
Salt and black pepper to taste
Stevia to taste (optional)

Makes 1-2 servings	
0 protein	
0 fat	
3 calories per serving	

Mix ingredients together. Marinate protein for 20 or more minutes.

HCG DIET *Tip*
Adjust the level of spices in a recipe to your personal taste. If you find a recipe has too much of a strong spice, adjust it to your palate.

Spicy Orange Sauce

Ingredients
½ orange, rolled and slightly juiced with rind
½ lemon, slightly juiced and with rind
½ cup water
1 tablespoon green onion, minced
1 clove garlic, crushed
¼ teaspoon ginger powder
¼ teaspoon garlic powder
Pinch of orange and lemon zest
Pinch of cayenne pepper
Stevia to taste

Makes 1-2 servings
(1 fruit)
.5 gram protein
1 fat
25 calories per serving

In a small saucepan add slightly juiced orange with rind and ½ lemon with rind to water. Bring to a boil, reduce heat and simmer, adding water as needed. Simmer until the pulp comes out of the rinds. Scrape out the pulp and discard the rinds. Continue stirring and reducing down the liquid by half until desired consistency is reached. Add onion, Stevia, and spices. Add chicken, white fish or beef and sauté or pour spicy orange sauce over desired cooked protein. Serve with remaining orange slices for garnish.

Tarragon and Garlic Infusion/Marinade

Ingredients
2-3 sprigs of fresh tarragon
½ cup of apple cider vinegar
2 tablespoons lemon juice
2 cloves of garlic, crushed and minced
1 tablespoon onion, diced
1 teaspoon salt
Fresh ground black or white pepper

Makes 1-2 servings
0 protein
0 fat
less than 5 calories

Pour vinegar and lemon juice into a lidded jar. Add sprigs of tarragon, garlic, onion, and spices. Marinate overnight or up to a week. Enjoy with fish, chicken, or as a marinade or dressing.

Tomato Basil Soup

Ingredients
2 cups chicken or vegetable broth (or substitute 1 cup water for 1 cup broth)
3 cups fresh tomatoes, chopped
3 ounces of tomato paste
4-6 leaves of fresh basil, rolled and sliced
1-2 cloves garlic, crushed and minced
2 tablespoons onion, chopped
1 teaspoon garlic powder
¼ teaspoon dried oregano
Pinch of marjoram
Salt and black pepper to taste

Makes 2 servings
(1 vegetable)
3 grams protein
2 grams fat
105 calories per serving

> Puree all ingredients in a food processor or blender. Pour into a saucepan and heat to a boil. Reduce heat and simmer for 20 to 30 minutes. Serve hot, garnish with fresh basil leaves or parsley.

Chicken and Cabbage Soup
(substitute beef and beef broth)

Ingredients
100 grams chicken
1 ½ cups cabbage
2 cups chicken broth (or substitute 1 cup water for 1 cup broth)
2 tablespoons Bragg's liquid aminos (optional)
2 cloves garlic, crushed and minced
1 tablespoon onion, chopped
¼ teaspoon thyme
¼ teaspoon rosemary
Cayenne pepper to taste
Salt and pepper to taste

Makes 1 serving
(1 protein, 1 vegetable)
28 grams protein
3 grams fat
225 calories

> Combine chicken and spices in medium saucepan. Bring broth to a boil. Add cabbage. Reduce heat and simmer for a minimum of 30 minutes. Add additional water to broth as needed. Variations: change the spices and add fresh tarragon or turmeric. Add ¼ lemon with rind to the broth and simmer for a rich lemon flavor.

Chicken Meatball Soup

Meatballs
Ingredients
100 grams ground chicken breast
1 teaspoon onion, minced
1 clove garlic, crushed and minced
Pinch of sage
Pinch of marjoram
Pinch of thyme
Dash of onion powder
Dash of garlic powder
1 serving Melba toast crumbs (optional)

Broth
Ingredients
2 cups chicken broth (or substitute 1 cup water for 1 cup broth)
2 tablespoons Bragg's liquid aminos
1 tablespoon apple cider vinegar
1 ½ cups celery or tomato, chopped (tomato adds an additional 25 calories)
1 tablespoon onion, chopped
2 cloves garlic, crushed and minced
1 bay leaf
Cayenne pepper to taste
Salt and pepper to taste

Combine ground chicken breast with spices, chopped garlic, onion, and crushed Melba toast. Form into balls. Bring broth to a boil, Add spices, vinegar, Bragg's liquid aminos, and chicken balls. Reduce to a simmer and cook a minimum of 30 minutes, adding the celery or tomato the last 5-10 minutes of cooking.

Makes 1 serving
(1 protein, 1 vegetable, 1 Melba toast)

28 grams protein

3 grams fat

185 calories

H C G DIET Tip *Supplement the soups with cabbage or other allowed vegetables and sip the broth slowly. You'll find that you can eat a lot of soup and maintain your 500 calories. The broth is very satisfying and filling. Make sure to account for the calories in the broth when calculating your 500 calories per day.*

Vegetable Beef Soup

Ingredients
100 grams lean beef, cubed
1 ½ cups celery, cabbage, or tomato, diced (cabbage or tomato adds an additional 25 calories)
2 cups beef or vegetable broth (or substitute 1 cup water for 1 cup of broth)
1 tablespoon onion, chopped
1 clove garlic, crushed and minced
1 bay leaf
1/8 teaspoon dried basil
1/8 teaspoon fresh or dried oregano
Pinch of thyme
Pinch of paprika
Pinch of chili powder
Salt and pepper to taste

> Combine onion, garlic, and spices with beef broth. Add celery and diced beef. Simmer for 20-30 minutes. Add tomatoes and simmer for an additional 5 minutes.

Makes 1 serving
(1 protein, 1 vegetable)

22 grams protein

9 grams fat

190 calories

PHASE 3 MODIFICATIONS: Add additional vegetables such as zucchini, bell peppers or a small amount of chopped carrots.

Savory Chicken Soup

Ingredients
100 grams chicken breast, cubed
1 ½ cups celery or tomatoes, chopped (tomatoes add 25 calories)
2 cups chicken broth (or substitute 1 cup water for 1 cup of broth)
1 tablespoon onion, minced
2 cloves garlic, crushed and sliced
1 bay leaf
½ teaspoon organic poultry spice blend
Cayenne pepper to taste
Salt and black pepper to taste

> Bring chicken stock to a boil. Add onion, garlic, and spices. Add chicken and vegetables and simmer on low heat for 20 minutes or more until chicken and cabbage are tender and fully cooked. Serve hot.
Sprinkle with chives or parsley if desired.

Makes 1 serving
(1 protein, 1 vegetable)

28 grams protein

3 grams fat

195 calories

Thai Beef Soup

Ingredients
100 grams beef
1 ½ cups celery
2 cups beef or vegetable broth (or substitute 1 cup water for 1 cup broth)
2 tablespoons Bragg's liquid aminos
1 tablespoon green onion, chopped
1 clove of garlic, crushed and minced
Fresh cilantro, chopped
½ teaspoon fresh ginger, grated
1/8 teaspoon chili powder or red pepper flakes
1 bay leaf
Pinch of cinnamon
Stevia to taste
Salt and pepper to taste

Makes 1 serving
(1 protein, 1 vegetable)
23 grams protein,
9 grams fat
190 calories

PHASE 3
MODIFICATIONS: Add chili or sesame oil and a few bean sprouts to the soup. Top with fresh sliced mushrooms.

Heat broth. Add dry spices, bay leaf, Bragg's, garlic, and onion, and bring to a boil. Reduce heat and simmer for 5 minutes. Add beef and celery and cook for 20 to 30 minutes until soft. Add salt, pepper, and Stevia. Garnish with fresh chopped cilantro.

Homemade Chicken Broth

Ingredients
3 large chicken breasts
10 or more cups of water
½ large onion, chopped
4 stalks of celery, chopped
5 cloves of garlic, sliced
1 bay leaf
Salt and pepper to taste

Makes multiple servings
.5 grams protein
0 fat
less than 10 calories per serving

In a large soup pot or crock pot combine chicken and 10 or more cups of water. Water should slightly cover the chicken. Add celery and spices. Heat to a boil then reduce heat to simmer. Allow to slow cook for 4 hours. Remove vegetables and chicken from broth. Refrigerate stock and skim off the chicken fat. Put through a strainer for a clear broth. Save the chicken and make **Chicken Salad** or add to soups.

HCG DIET Tip *Eating soups may help curb any hunger you might be experiencing especially at the beginning of the 500 calorie VLCD phase of the diet.*

Homemade Vegetable Broth

Ingredients
10 or more cups of water
½ large onion, chopped
6-10 stalks celery
10 cloves of garlic, chopped
2 bay leaves
1 teaspoon paprika
1 teaspoon garlic powder
1 teaspoon basil
1 teaspoon of thyme
Salt and pepper to taste

> Bring water to a boil in a large soup pot or crock-pot. Add vegetables and spices. Slow cook for 2-4 hours. Strain out vegetables and cool. Use as a base for soups.

Makes multiple servings
0 protein
0 fat
less than 5 calories

Fennel Soup

Ingredients
1 ½ cups fennel bulb, chopped
2 cups chicken or vegetable broth (or substitute 1 cup water for 1 cup broth)
1 tablespoon onion, finely minced
¼ teaspoon allspice seasoning blend
Salt and pepper to taste

> Add chopped fennel bulbs, spices, and minced onion to vegetable broth. Heat in small saucepan and simmer for 20 minutes. Add lemon with rind to the broth if desired. Serve warm with chopped sprigs of fennel for garnish.

Makes 1 serving
(1 vegetable)
1 gram protein
0 fat
45 calories

PHASE 3
MODIFICATIONS: Add half and half or cream.

Celery Soup

Ingredients
1 ½ cups celery, chopped (may use celery from crock pot cooking or 1 baked celery recipe)
2 cups chicken broth (or substitute 1 cup water for 1 cup broth)
¼ teaspoon thyme
1 bay leaf
¼ teaspoon dried basil
Salt and pepper to taste

Makes 1 serving
(1 vegetable)
1.5 grams protein
.5 grams fat
55 calories

▶ Cook celery until very soft or use crock-pot or vegetable broth cooked celery. Puree in a food processor or blender with broth and spices. Simmer in a saucepan for 20-30 minutes.

Chili

Ingredients
100 grams lean ground beef (less than 7% fat)
1 ½ cups tomatoes, chopped
½ cup water
1 tablespoon onion, minced
2 cloves garlic, crushed and minced
Pinch of garlic powder
Pinch of onion powder
¼ teaspoon chili powder
Pinch of oregano
Cayenne pepper to taste (optional)
Salt and pepper to taste

Makes 1 serving
(1 protein, 1 vegetable)
23 grams protein
8 grams fat
195 calories

PHASE 3
MODIFICATIONS: Top with cheddar cheese and a dollop of sour cream.

▶ Brown ground beef in small frying pan, add onions and garlic. Stir in tomatoes and water. Add spices and simmer slowly until liquid is reduced. The longer it cooks, the more tender and flavorful it will be. Add a little water as needed to prevent burning. Serve with chopped green onion or tomato garnish and salt and pepper to taste.

HCG DIET Tip *Make bundles of fresh herbs to add to soups or create herb infusions by immersing them in lemon juice or vinegar. You can use these on salads or as a marinade.*

Lemony Spinach and Chicken Soup

Ingredients
100 grams chicken
2 cups chicken broth (or substitute 1 cup water for 1 cup broth)
½ lemon with rind
1-2 cups loosely packed spinach, cut into strips
1 tablespoon onion, chopped
1 clove garlic, crushed and minced
1 stalk lemongrass (optional)
¼ teaspoon thyme or to taste
Cayenne pepper to taste
Salt and pepper to taste

Makes 1 serving
(1 protein, 1 vegetable)

26 grams protein

3 grams fat

190 calories

> Lightly brown the chicken in small saucepan with a little lemon juice. Add the onion, garlic, spices, and chicken broth. Add lemon with rind and simmer for 20-30 minutes. Add the fresh spinach during the last five minutes of cooking. Serve and enjoy.

Asparagus Soup

Ingredients
1 ½ cups asparagus, chopped
2 cups chicken or vegetable broth (or substitute 1 cup water for 1 cup broth)
2 tablespoons Bragg's liquid aminos
2 tablespoons onion, chopped
¼ teaspoon thyme
¼ teaspoon garlic powder
¼ teaspoon onion powder
1 bay leaf
1 tablespoon milk (optional)
Salt and pepper to taste
Old Bay seasoning to taste

Makes 1 serving
(1 vegetable)

5 grams protein

.5 grams fat

95 calories

PHASE 3
MODIFICATIONS:
Sauté the onion in a little butter, add sliced mushrooms, cheddar cheese and cream or half and half to the soup.

> Trim asparagus to remove the tough ends of the stalk and steam until soft. Puree asparagus with broth and spices in a blender or food processor. Heat soup in a saucepan and enjoy. Add 100 grams diced chicken if desired. You can replace dried spices with 1-2 teaspoons of Old Bay seasoning if you wish.

Spicy Chilled Tomato Soup

Ingredients
1 ½ cups tomatoes
1 tablespoon apple cider vinegar
1 tablespoon lemon juice
1 tablespoon green onion, sliced
1 garlic clove, crushed and minced
Dash of mustard powder
3 leaves fresh basil, rolled and minced
Pinch of cayenne pepper
Salt and fresh ground black pepper to taste

Makes 2 servings
(1 vegetable)

3 grams protein

0 fat

55 calories

> Combine tomatoes, vinegar, lemon juice, and spices. Puree in a food processor and chill for 1 hour before serving.

Hot and Sour Chicken Soup

Ingredients
100 grams chicken breast, diced
1 cup chicken broth
1 cup water
4 tablespoons apple cider vinegar
2 tablespoons Bragg's liquid aminos
½ lemon in quarters with rind
1 clove garlic, crushed and minced
2 tablespoons onion, minced
Cayenne pepper to taste
Pinch of chili powder or red chili flakes
Salt and pepper to taste
Stevia to taste (optional)

Makes 1 serving
(1 protein)

25 grams protein

2 grams fat

150 calories

PHASE 3
MODIFICATIONS:
Add a small amount of fresh pineapple juice. Add vegetables such as zucchini, cauliflower, small amount of carrots, etc. Add a little chili oil or paste to the soup for added heat and flavor.

> Boil lemon wedges with rind in 1 cup of water until pulp comes out of the rind. Scrape out additional pulp and juice. Add the diced chicken, spices and chicken broth. Simmer until cooked.

Variation: You can add orange juice as an option and your choice of approved vegetable or substitute shrimp for chicken.

Creole Gumbo (enjoy with shrimp or chicken)

Ingredients
100 grams shrimp or 1 **Chicken Sausage** recipe
2 cups vegetable broth (or substitute 1 cup water for 1 cup broth)
1 ½ cups tomatoes, chopped
2 tablespoons tomato paste
2 tablespoons green or white onion
2 cloves of garlic, crushed and minced
2 tablespoons apple cider vinegar
Dash of Worcestershire sauce
Liquid smoke hickory smoke flavoring to taste
Cayenne pepper to taste
Salt and pepper to taste

Makes 1 serving
(1 protein, 1 vegetable)

24 grams protein

2 grams fat

210 calories

PHASE 3
MODIFICATIONS: Add additional mixed protein ingredients like crab, chicken, or sausage. Add additional vegetables such as okra, celery, and bell pepper. Enjoy with a dollop of sour cream.

> Fry shrimp or chicken sausage in a saucepan with onions. Add tomato paste, tomatoes, and broth. Mix well. Add the spices and vinegar. Simmer for 20-30 minutes. Serve hot and garnish with fresh parsley.

Middle Eastern Vegetable Soup

Ingredients
2 cups vegetable broth (or substitute 1 cup water for 1 cup broth)
1 ½ cups tomatoes or celery, chopped (tomatoes add 25 calories)
8 ounces tomato sauce or 3 ounces tomato paste (omit if celery is used)
1 clove garlic, crushed and minced
1 tablespoon onion, chopped
1/8 teaspoon ginger
¼ teaspoon cumin
Salt and black pepper to taste
Fresh parsley, cilantro or mint

Makes 1 serving
(1 vegetable)

4 grams protein

0 fat

110 calories

PHASE 3
MODIFICATIONS: Add string beans, zucchini or other vegetables as desired.

> Combine broth, tomato sauce, and paste. Bring to a boil. Reduce heat and add spices. Simmer for 20-30 minutes or until vegetables are tender.

Crab Bisque

Ingredients
100 grams crab meat
1 cup tomatoes, chopped
2 cups vegetable broth (or substitute 1 cup water for 1 cup broth)
1 tablespoon onion, minced
1 clove garlic, crushed and minced
1 teaspoon Old Bay seasoning
1 bay leaf
1 tablespoon milk (optional)
Cayenne pepper to taste
Salt and black pepper to taste

▷ Puree tomatoes and broth in a food processor or blender. Heat up mixture in a small saucepan. Add the crab and spices and simmer for 20-30 minutes, stirring frequently.

Makes 1 serving
(1 protein, 1 vegetable)
24 grams protein
2 grams fat
175 calories

PHASE 3
MODIFICATIONS: Add half and half or cream.

Sweet Strawberry Soup (serve hot or cold)

Ingredients
5 large strawberries
2 tablespoons lemon juice
1 tablespoon milk
¼ cup water
Vanilla liquid Stevia or powdered vanilla to taste
Dash of cinnamon

▷ Puree strawberries with spices, lemon juice, water and milk. Heat the strawberry mixture in a small saucepan for 3-5 minutes. Serve hot or chilled with a garnish of mint.

Makes one serving
(1 fruit)
.5 grams protein
0 fat
30 calories

PHASE 3
MODIFICATIONS: Add 3 tablespoons cream cheese, half and half, or cream. Omit the lemon juice. Top with a sprinkle of chopped roasted nuts.

ot and Sour Thai Shrimp Soup

Ingredients
100 grams shrimp
2 cups vegetable broth (or substitute 1 cup water for 1 cup broth)
Juice of ½ lemon with rind
1 lemon grass stalk
2-3 slices of fresh ginger
Red pepper flakes or cayenne pepper to taste
1 tablespoon green onion
1 tablespoon fresh cilantro, chopped
Salt and pepper to taste

Makes 1 serving
(1 protein)

20 grams protein

2 grams fat

125 calories

PHASE 3
MODIFICATIONS: Add
straw mushrooms and
fish paste. Add a little hot
chili paste or chili oil.

> Bring the broth to a boil. Add the ginger, lemongrass, lemon juice, onion, and pepper. Simmer for 10-15 minutes. Add the shrimp and cilantro and cook another 8 minutes. Serve hot. Remove lemongrass before serving.

French Onion Soup

Ingredients
2 cups beef broth (or substitute one cup water for one cup broth)
1 Melba toast crumbled or **Melba Croutons** (optional)
1 teaspoon Worcestershire sauce
1 tablespoon Bragg's liquid aminos (optional)
1 tablespoon lemon juice
¼ to ½ onion in thin strips
1 clove garlic, crushed and minced
Stevia to taste
Salt and black pepper to taste

Makes 1-2 servings
(1 vegetable, 1 Melba
toast)

1 gram protein

1 gram fat

50 calories

PHASE 3
MODIFICATIONS: Top
with mozzarella or
provolone cheese.

> Brown the onions in a little water and lemon juice. Add beef broth and spices and simmer for 20-30 minutes. Top with **Melba Croutons**.

Albondigas Soup (Mexican Meatball Soup)

Meatballs
Ingredients
100 grams lean ground beef
1 serving Melba toast crumbs
Dash of onion powder
Dash of garlic powder
1/8 teaspoon oregano
1 teaspoon onion, minced
1clove garlic, crushed and minced
Pinch of cumin
Cayenne pepper to taste
Salt and pepper to taste

Broth
Ingredients
1 cup beef broth
1 cup water
1 ½ cups fresh tomatoes or celery
1 tablespoon onion, chopped
1 clove garlic, crushed and minced
1 tablespoon fresh cilantro, chopped
¼ teaspoon dried oregano
Salt and pepper to taste

Make meatballs by mixing ground beef, Melba crumbs, finely diced onion, garlic, powdered spices, and chopped cilantro. Form into balls and drop into beef broth. Add spices, onion and garlic to the broth and bring to a boil. Reduce to a simmer and cook for a minimum of 30 minutes. Add your choice of celery or tomato to the broth in the last 10 minutes of cooking. Garnish with fresh chopped cilantro and oregano.

Makes 1 serving
(1 protein, 1 vegetable,
1 Melba toast)

24 grams protein

8 grams fat

230 calories

PHASE 3
MODIFICATIONS: Add
additional vegetables
such as zucchini or a
small amount of carrots.

H C G
DIET
Tip

Choosing to make your own chicken, beef, and vegetable broths will allow you to control the sodium and types of vegetables used in the broth. Always read labels to ensure that you are not ingesting fat, sugar, MSG, or excess sodium if you use packaged broths. You can substitute one cup of water for one cup of broth in any of my recipes to help control the calories or sodium if you wish.

Chicken Curry

Ingredients
100 grams chicken, cubed
¼ cup chicken broth or water
¼ teaspoon curry powder or to taste
Pinch of turmeric
Dash of garlic powder
Dash of onion powder
1 tablespoon onion, minced
Salt and pepper to taste
Stevia to taste
Cayenne to taste

Makes 1 serving
(1 protein)
26 grams protein
2 grams fat
145 calories

> Dissolve spices in chicken broth in a small saucepan. Add chopped
onion, garlic and chicken. Add Stevia to taste for a more sweet curry.
Sauté chicken in liquid until fully cooked and liquid is reduced by half.
Additional water may be added to achieve desired consistency. Serve hot
or cold.

Oriental Ginger Chicken

Ingredients
100 grams chicken
¼ cup chicken broth or water
4 tablespoons lemon juice
¼ teaspoon lemon or orange zest
½ teaspoon fresh ginger
1 tablespoon Bragg's liquid aminos
1 tablespoon onion, chopped
Stevia to taste
Cayenne pepper to taste
Salt and pepper to taste

Makes 1 serving
(1 protein)
26 grams protein
2 grams fat
155 calories

> In a small sauce pan, sauté chicken in a little lemon juice and water
until slightly browned. Add spices, ginger, salt, lemon, and Stevia.
Add Bragg's liquid aminos and cook thoroughly. Deglaze the pan
periodically by adding a little water. Serve hot and garnish with lemon or
orange slices.

Chicken Pesto

Ingredients
100 grams chicken breast, thinly sliced or whole
3 tablespoons lemon juice
Salt and pepper to taste

Pesto

Ingredients
3 cloves raw garlic
¼ cup fresh basil leaves
1 tablespoon apple cider vinegar
¼ cup chicken broth or water
2 tablespoons lemon juice
¼ teaspoon dried oregano
Salt and black pepper to taste

Marinate chicken in lemon juice, salt, and pepper. Fry in a pan until lightly browned and cooked thoroughly. For the pesto sauce, puree fresh basil, garlic, chicken broth, and lemon juice in a food processor. Add pesto mixture to chicken, add a little water, and cook on medium heat coating chicken with pesto mixture. Add salt and pepper to taste and serve hot. Pesto sauce may be made by itself and added to vegetables or other protein options.

Makes
(1 protein) Makes 2-3
servings of pesto sauce.

26 grams protein

2 grams fat

140 calories

PHASE 3
MODIFICATIONS: Add ¼ cup pine nuts or walnuts and ¼ cup parmesan cheese to the food processor along with ¼ cup of olive oil. For a creamy pesto, add a little half and half and omit the lemon juice.

Chicken Tarragon

Ingredients
100 grams chicken breast
¼ cup **Tarragon and Garlic Infusion**
¼ cup chicken broth or water
2 tablespoons lemon juice
½ teaspoon fresh tarragon, chopped
1 tablespoon onion, chopped
1 clove garlic, minced
Dash of mustard powder
Salt and pepper to taste

Makes 1 serving
(1 protein)

26 grams protein

2 grams fat

150 calories

Heat the chicken broth, vinegar, garlic, and onion in a small saucepan or frying pan. Add chicken and sauté for about 10 minutes or until chicken is completely cooked and liquid is reduced. Deglaze the pan periodically with a little water to create a sauce. Serve hot.

pple Sausage

C Ground chicken breast
 oons apple, minced
 ng Melba toast crumbs (optional)
 ablespoons chicken broth or water
2 tablespoons apple juice
1 tablespoon onion, finely minced
Dash of garlic powder
Dash of onion powder
Dash of cinnamon
Dash of clove or nutmeg (optional)
Dash of cayenne to taste
Stevia to taste (optional)
Salt and black pepper to taste

Makes 1 serving
(1 protein, 1 fruit,
1 Melba toast)

26 grams protein

2 grams fat

190 calories

> Combine ground chicken, diced apple, and dry spices in a small bowl.
> Add in the minced onion and apple juice and mix thoroughly. Form
> into 2-3 round patties and fry in chicken broth until fully cooked and
lightly brown. Deglaze periodically with a little water to intensify the
flavors and keep the patties moist.

Chicken Asparagus Bake

Ingredients
100 grams chicken, cubed
1 ½ cups asparagus, chopped
½ cup chicken broth or water
1 Melba toast, crushed (optional)
1 clove garlic, crushed and minced
2 tablespoons onion, chopped
Dash of paprika
Salt and pepper to taste

Makes 1 serving
(1 protein, 1 vegetable,
1 Melba toast)

30 grams protein

3 grams fat

225 calories

> Place chicken, asparagus, liquids, and spices into small baking dish.
> Bake at 375 degrees for 30 minutes or until bubbly and hot. Top with
> crushed Melba toast crumbs and sprinkle with paprika.

Sweet Lemon Chicken

Ingredients
100 grams chicken, thinly sliced
½ lemon with rind
1 tablespoon Bragg's liquid aminos
¼ cup chicken broth or water
1 cup water
Dash of cayenne pepper
Salt to taste
Stevia to taste (optional)

Makes 1 serving
(1 protein)
26 grams protein
2 grams fat
150 calories

Slice ½ lemon in quarters and add to water. In a small saucepan boil lemon quarters until pulp comes out of the rind. Add broth, chicken, Bragg's, and spices and simmer on low heat until chicken is cooked and sauce is reduced by half. Deglaze periodically with water if necessary. Garnish with fresh lemon slices, lemon zest or mint.

Rosemary Chicken

Ingredients
100 grams chicken breast, thick sliced or whole
1 serving Melba toast crumbs
¼ cup chicken broth or water
3 tablespoons lemon juice
½ teaspoon fresh rosemary
¼ teaspoon onion powder
¼ teaspoon garlic powder
Salt and pepper to taste
Pinch of lemon zest

Makes 1 serving
(1 protein, 1 Melba toast)
3 grams protein
2 grams fat
165 calories

Marinate chicken in lemon juice, salt, and rosemary. Mix spices and Melba toast crumbs together in shallow bowl or plate. Coat the chicken pieces with spice mixture and place in baking dish. Add broth and top chicken with additional spice mixture. Bake chicken at 350 degrees for approximately 20 minutes or until cooked. Sprinkle chicken with lemon juice, salt, and pepper to taste. Garnish with fresh chopped parsley and lemon slices.

Chicken Tacos

Ingredients
100 grams chicken breast, finely chopped or ground
¼ cup chicken broth or water
1 tablespoon onion, chopped
1 clove garlic, crushed and minced
1/8 teaspoon oregano
Cayenne pepper to taste
Pinch of cumin
Fresh cilantro, chopped
2-4 large lettuce leaves

Makes 1 serving
(1 protein, 1 vegetable)
25 grams protein
2 grams fat
155 calories

> In a small frying pan cook chicken in broth. Add onion, garlic, and spices. Deglaze pan with lemon juice or a little water. Serve chicken taco style in butter lettuce or romaine leaves or top with **Salsa**.

Tomato Basil Chicken

Ingredients
100 grams chicken, cubed
1 ½ cups tomatoes, chopped
¼ cup chicken broth or water
2 tablespoons lemon juice
2 tablespoons onion, chopped
1-2 cloves garlic, sliced
3 leaves basil, rolled and sliced
1/8 teaspoon oregano fresh or dried
Dash of garlic powder
Dash of onion powder
Cayenne to taste
Salt and pepper to taste

Makes 1 serving
(1 protein, 1 vegetable)
29 grams protein
3 grams fat
200 calories

> Lightly brown the chicken in small saucepan with lemon juice. Add garlic, onion, spices, and water. After chicken is cooked, add fresh tomatoes and basil. Continue cooking for 5-10 minutes. Salt and pepper to taste, garnish with fresh basil.

HCG DIET Tip
Weigh out individual 100 grams of meat, chicken or fish, put in plastic bags and freeze for later use. Freeze individual servings pre-seasoned with marinades or spice blends for added flavor. This saves time when preparing meals.

Sweet Mustard Chicken

Ingredients
100 grams chicken breast
¼ cup chicken broth or water
1 tablespoon Bragg's liquid aminos
1/8 teaspoon mustard powder or to taste
¼ teaspoon fresh ginger or sprinkle of ginger powder
1 tablespoon onion, chopped
½ teaspoon garlic powder
Salt and pepper to taste
Stevia to taste

Makes 1 serving
(1 protein)
26 grams protein
2 grams fat
145 calories

Dissolve spices in chicken broth. Add chicken, broth, and onion, to a small saucepan and cook on medium heat for about 5-10 minutes or until chicken is tender. Periodically deglaze the pan with a little water to create a richer sauce.

Chicken Cacciatore

Ingredients
100 grams chicken breast, diced
1 ½ cups tomatoes, chopped
¼ cup chicken broth or water
2 tablespoons tomato paste
1 tablespoon apple cider vinegar
2 tablespoons lemon juice
1 tablespoon Bragg's liquid aminos
2 tablespoons onion, chopped
2 cloves garlic, crushed and minced
¼ teaspoon onion powder
¼ teaspoon garlic powder
1 bay leaf
Pinch of cayenne to taste
Stevia to taste

Makes 1 serving
(1 protein, 1 vegetable)
30 grams protein
3 grams fat
127 calories

Brown the chicken with garlic, onion, and lemon juice in a small saucepan. Deglaze the pan with the chicken broth. Add tomatoes, tomato paste, vinegar, and spices. Simmer on low heat for 20 minutes, stirring occasionally. Remove the bay leaf and serve hot.

Sweet and Sour Chicken

Ingredients
100 grams chicken breast
½ orange, ½ lemon with rind
1 cup water
1 tablespoon Bragg's liquid aminos
2 tablespoons apple cider vinegar
1 tablespoon onion, minced
1 tablespoon lemon and/or orange zest
Dash of garlic powder
Dash of onion powder
1 tablespoon hot sauce
Cayenne pepper to taste
Stevia to taste
Salt and pepper to taste

Makes 1 serving
(1 protein, 1 fruit)

26 grams protein

2 grams fat

190 calories

PHASE 3
MODIFICATIONS:
Add a small amount of
fresh pineapple, bell
pepper, and chopped
mushrooms.

In a frying pan or small saucepan place ½ orange and ½ lemon with the rinds in water and boil until pulp comes out of the rind. Remove rinds from the water and scrape out remaining pulp and juice with a spoon. Add spices, onion, and Stevia to taste. Add chicken and cook until liquid is reduced by approximately half and desired consistency is achieved. Add onion and garlic powders which act as slight thickening agent. Serve hot and garnish with lemon.

Chicken Paprika

Ingredients
100 grams chicken
½ cup chicken broth or water
3 tablespoons tomato paste
1 teaspoon paprika
1 tablespoon red onion, chopped
1 clove garlic, crushed and minced
1 bay leaf
Salt and pepper to taste

Makes 1 serving
(1 protein, 1 vegetable)

25 grams protein

3 grams fat

172 calories

PHASE 3
MODIFICATIONS: Sauté
the chicken in a little
butter or olive oil, then
add tomato, broth, and
¼ cup sour cream.

Combine broth, chicken, garlic, and onion. Stir in tomato paste and spices. Simmer chicken mixture for 20 minutes or more. Serve with sliced tomatoes and garnish with parsley.

Stuffed Chicken Rolls

Ingredients
100 grams chicken breast
2 cups spinach, chopped
½ cup chicken broth or water
1 tablespoon onion, chopped
1 clove of garlic, crushed and minced
1 tablespoon lemon juice
Dash of onion powder
Dash of garlic powder
Pinch of cayenne pepper
Salt and pepper to taste

▶ Tenderize chicken manually by pounding until flat. Cook spinach lightly with garlic, onion, and spices. Strain out excess liquid from the spinach and place mound of spinach in the center of the pounded chicken. Roll up the spinach mixture inside the chicken breast. Place rolls in baking dish and add chicken broth to the pan. Bake the rolls in 350 degree oven for about 15 minutes or until chicken is cooked completely.

Makes 1 serving
(1 protein, 1 vegetable)

28 grams protein	
3 grams fat	
180 calories	

PHASE 3
MODIFICATIONS: Brush chicken with olive oil, add marinara sauce, and top with mozzarella cheese if desired. Bake until brown and bubbly. Another modification is to mix the spinach mixture with ricotta cheese or sliced mushrooms.

Oregano Chicken

Ingredients
100 grams chicken breast
1 teaspoon dried oregano or 1 tablespoon fresh finely minced
1 serving Melba toast crumbs (optional)
¼ cup chicken broth or water
¼ teaspoon garlic powder
¼ teaspoon onion powder
Salt and pepper to taste

▶ Crush Melba toast into fine powder and mix with dried spices. Dip chicken breast in chicken broth and coat with Melba spice mixture.
Layer in baking dish and add remaining broth to the bottom. Bake in 350 degree oven for 15-20 minutes until crusty brown on top. Add a little water if necessary to keep chicken from burning.

Makes 1 serving
(1 protein, 1 Melba toast)

25 grams protein	
2 grams fat	
160 calories	

PHASE 3
MODIFICATIONS: Dip chicken in egg and coat with herbed Melba toast or parmesan cheese. Fry with a little olive oil. Top with marinara sauce and cheese or a lemon butter sauce and parmesan.

Bruschetta Chicken

Ingredients
100 grams chicken breast, thick sliced or whole
1 Melba toast, crushed into crumbs
2 medium Roma tomatoes, diced
2 tablespoons lemon juice
1 tablespoon Bragg's liquid aminos
2 tablespoons apple cider vinegar
2 cloves garlic, finely chopped
3 large fresh basil leaves, rolled and sliced
Pinch of dried oregano
Pinch of marjoram
Salt and black pepper to taste

Makes 1 serving
(1 protein, 1 vegetable, 1 Melba toast)

29 grams protein

2 grams fat

210 calories

PHASE 3
MODIFICATIONS: Brush chicken breasts with olive oil and substitute balsamic vinegar (check the sugar count) for the bruschetta. Serve with fresh grated parmesan cheese or lay a slice of provolone cheese over the breast then top with bruschetta sauce.

> Marinate chicken in lemon juice, Bragg's, vinegar, salt, and pepper. Mix Melba crumbs with dry spices. Coat the chicken in Melba crumbs/herb mixture and fry chicken in small pan until golden brown. Deglaze the pan periodically with a little broth to keep chicken from burning. For the bruschetta sauce, chop tomatoes finely and put into small bowl. Roll basil leaves together, crush lightly, and cut horizontally to create fine slices. Mix ingredients together with lemon juice, vinegar, and salt and pepper to taste. Serve chilled bruschetta sauce over the hot chicken.

Barbecued Chicken

Ingredients
100 grams of chicken breast, whole
1 serving of **Barbecue Sauce**

Makes 1 serving
(1 protein, 1 vegetable)

26 grams protein

2 grams fat

173 calories

> Coat chicken with barbeque sauce and fry with a little water in small frying pan until cooked thoroughly on low heat. Stir constantly and add water so that it doesn't burn on grill on the barbeque. Serve hot. Add salt and pepper to taste.

Moroccan Lemon Chicken

Ingredients
100 grams chicken breast
Juice of ½ lemon
1 tablespoon onion, minced
Pinch of ginger
Pinch of ground coriander
Pinch of saffron
Pinch of lemon zest
Salt and pepper to taste
Lemon slices

Makes 1 serving
(1 protein)

25 grams protein

2 grams fat

142 calories

Marinate saffron strands in lemon juice, then crush into a paste.
Add dry spices. Dip chicken breast in lemon juice and spice mixture.
Rub additional spices into chicken breast with salt and pepper. Wrap individual servings in foil and cover with slices of lemon and a little of the saffron mixture. Bake chicken at 350 degrees for 20-30 minutes or until chicken is cooked completely and tender.

Buffalo Style Chicken Fingers

Ingredients
100 grams of chicken, cut into long thin strips
Melba toast, crushed (optional)
2 tablespoons hot sauce (Frank's red hot sauce works the best for this recipe)
4 tablespoons lemon juice
Salt and black pepper to taste

Makes 1 serving
(1 protein, 1 Melba toast)

25 grams protein

2 grams fat

157 calories

Marinate chicken strips in lemon juice and salt. Coat chicken strips with Melba crumbs. Fry in frying pan until lightly browned and cooked thoroughly. Toss with hot sauce and black pepper to taste. Serve as finger food or as an entrée. Serve with raw celery sticks or desired vegetable. Garnish with parsley.

Baked Apple Chicken

Ingredients
100 grams chicken, cubed
½ apple, finely chopped
2 tablespoons lemon juice
1 tablespoon apple cider vinegar
1/8 teaspoon cinnamon
Salt and pepper to taste
Stevia to taste
Dash of cayenne

Makes 1 serving
(1 protein, 1 fruit)

25 grams protein

2 grams fat

177 calories

▶ Lightly brown the chicken in lemon juice. Add chopped apple and evenly coat with a mixture of apple cider vinegar, lemon juice, Stevia, cinnamon, cayenne, and pinch of salt. Put in small baking dish and add additional vinegar and lemon juice. Bake the chicken at 350 degrees for 25 minutes or until cooked completely. Serve with the rest of the apple in thin slices on the side.

Orange Glazed Chicken Breast

Ingredients
100 grams chicken
One serving **Spicy Orange Sauce** or **Sweet Orange Marinade**

Makes 1 serving
(1 protein, 1 fruit)

25 grams protein

2 grams fat

155 calories

▶ Prepare orange sauce. Cook the chicken with the sauce in small saucepan with the juices or bake in oven at 375 degrees for approximately 20 minutes or until cooked thoroughly. In a small saucepan reduce liquid until desired consistency. Deglaze the pan periodically by adding water and pour remaining mixture over chicken breast.

HCG DIET *Tip* *Use small amounts of garlic or onion powder as a slight thickening agent for dressings and sauces. Check the label to avoid added starches and sugars in any spices.*

Roasted Garlic Chicken

Ingredients
100 grams chicken, sliced
1 serving Melba toast crumbs
¼ cup chicken broth or water
2 tablespoons lemon juice
1 teaspoon Bragg's liquid aminos
2 cloves of garlic, sliced
¼ teaspoon onion powder
½ teaspoon garlic powder
Salt and pepper to taste

Makes 1 serving
(1 protein 1 Melba toast)

26 grams protein

2 grams fat

165 calories

PHASE 3
MODIFICATIONS: Baste chicken breast with olive oil. Add parmesan cheese to the coating.

▶ Marinate chicken in liquid ingredients. Add dry spices to Melba toast crumbs and coat chicken with the herbed mixture. Place chicken in a small baking dish and add marinade to the bottom. Cover the chicken breast with slices of garlic and bake in 375 degree oven for 20 minutes or until thoroughly cooked and lightly brown. Garnish with chopped parsley.

Savory Baked Chicken

Ingredients
100 grams chicken breast
1 serving Melba toast crumbs
½ cup chicken broth or water
2 tablespoons lemon juice
1 tablespoon Bragg's liquid aminos
¼ teaspoon onion powder
¼ teaspoon garlic powder
1/8 teaspoon thyme
Pinch of fresh or dried rosemary
1 teaspoon fresh parsley, chopped
Salt and pepper to taste

Makes 1 serving
(1 protein, 1 Melba toast)

26 grams protein

3 grams fat

165 calories

PHASE 3
MODIFICATIONS: Dip chicken in egg, add grated parmesan cheese to the spice mixture, and drizzle with olive oil.

▶ Combine Melba crumbs with dried spices. Dip chicken breast in lemon juice and Bragg's liquid aminos and coat with herb mixture.
Bake chicken in 350 degree oven for approximately 20 minutes or until thoroughly cooked.

Mexican Style Cilantro Chicken

Ingredients
100 grams chicken, cubed or sliced
1 ½ cups tomatoes, chopped
½ cup chicken broth or water
2 tablespoons lemon juice
Fresh cilantro, chopped
1 tablespoon onion, chopped
¼ teaspoon dried oregano
¼ clove fresh garlic, minced
¼ teaspoon chili powder
Cayenne pepper to taste
Pinch of cumin
Salt and pepper to taste

Makes 1 serving
(1 protein 1 vegetable)

29 grams protein

3 grams fat

200 calories

> Lightly brown the chicken with a little lemon juice. Add spices, additional lemon juice, and chicken broth. When the chicken is cooked thoroughly, add fresh tomatoes and cilantro and cook for 5-10 more minutes.

Spicy Chicken Sausage Patties

Ingredients
100 grams chicken breast, ground (must be breast meat, no dark meat)
Dash of onion powder
Dash of garlic powder
1 tablespoon onion, minced
1 clove of garlic, crushed and minced
Cayenne pepper to taste
Salt and pepper to taste

Makes 1 serving
(1 protein)

25 grams protein

2 grams fat

142 calories

> Mix ingredients thoroughly in small bowl. Form mixture into 2 or 3 patties and fry in small saucepan deglazing periodically with water to enhance flavor and keep chicken moist. Cook thoroughly until lightly browned.

Middle Eastern Spiced Chicken

Ingredients
100 grams chicken
1 ½ cups fresh tomatoes, chopped
½ cup chicken broth or water
3 tablespoons lemon juice
1 tablespoon onion, minced
1 clove garlic, crushed and minced
1/8 teaspoon fresh ginger, grated
¼ teaspoon allspice
Dash of cumin
Dash of cinnamon
Salt and black pepper to taste

Makes 1 serving
(1 protein 1 vegetable)
Make multiple servings
using whole 100 gram
chicken breast pieces.

29 grams protein

2 grams fat

200 calories

▶ Combine spices with liquid ingredients. Bring to a boil. Add tomatoes
and chicken to the sauce. Simmer for 20-30 minutes and serve.

Szechwan Chicken with Cabbage

Ingredients
100 grams chicken breast
1 ½ cups cabbage, chopped
1 cup chicken broth or water
2 tablespoons Bragg's liquid aminos
1 teaspoon hot sauce
Pinch of crushed red pepper flakes
Pinch of fresh or powdered ginger
1 clove garlic, crushed and minced
1 tablespoon green onion, chopped
Stevia to taste

Makes 1 serving
(1 protein, 1 vegetable)

28 grams protein

2 grams fat

200 calories

▶ Brown chicken in Bragg's and a little water. Add chicken broth and
spices. Simmer for 5 minutes. Add the cabbage and allow to cook for
10 minutes or until cabbage is tender. Add additional water if
necessary. Top with additional green onions for garnish and sprinkle
with lemon juice and additional Bragg's.

H C G
DIET
Tip

*"Deglaze" a recipe
by allowing the
meat, spices, and
liquids to reduce
until the pan is
dry and starting
to brown. Add
a small amount
of water or broth
to create a rich,
flavorful sauce for
your dish.*

Crock-Pot Chicken

Ingredients
Several 100 gram whole chicken breast pieces
½ cup onion, chopped
5 cloves fresh garlic, chopped
1 teaspoon paprika
½ teaspoon cayenne
1 teaspoon onion powder
½ teaspoon thyme
1 teaspoon garlic powder
1 teaspoon whole black peppercorns
Salt and pepper to taste

Makes 1 serving
(1 protein)
25 grams protein
2 grams fat
145 calories per serving

> Place pieces of chicken in crock-pot and cover with enough water so it doesn't burn. Add spices and onion. Cook on medium for 3 or more hours. Save the juices for sauces and dressings. Variations: add 1 can tomato paste or fresh chopped tomatoes. Try an organic poultry spice mixture for a rich sage flavor.

Cinnamon Chicken

Ingredients
100 grams of chicken
1 serving Melba toast crumbs
½ cup chicken broth or water
¼ teaspoon ground cinnamon
Pinch of nutmeg
Pinch of cardamom
1/8 teaspoon curry powder
Dash of garlic powder
Salt and pepper to taste
Stevia to taste

Makes 1 serving
(1 protein, 1 Melba toast)
25 grams protein
2 grams fat
167 calories

> Mix Melba toast crumbs with ½ of the dry spices in a small bowl. Dip chicken in broth and coat with Melba spice mixture. Lay out 100 gram servings in shallow baking dish. Add broth and mix in the rest of the spices. Top the chicken with the rest of the Melba spice mixture. Bake chicken at 350 degrees for 20 minutes or until chicken is fully cooked.

Tangy Vinegar Chicken

Ingredients
100 grams chicken breast
¼ cup chicken broth or water
¼ cup apple cider vinegar
2 tablespoons lemon juice
1 tablespoon onion, chopped
1 clove garlic, diced
Salt and pepper to taste

Makes 1 serving
(1 protein)

25 grams protein

2 grams fat

145 calories

> In a small saucepan combine vinegar, chicken stock, onion, garlic, salt, and pepper. Add chicken and cook thoroughly. Deglaze the pan periodically with a little water to create a sauce.

Spicy Mustard Chicken

Ingredients
100 grams chicken
½ cup chicken broth or water
2 tablespoons lemon juice
1 tablespoon **Homemade Mustard**
¼ teaspoon dried basil
1/8 teaspoon tarragon
Salt and pepper to taste
Stevia to taste

Makes 1 serving
(1 protein)

25 grams protein

2 grams fat

147 calories

> Lightly sauté the chicken in chicken broth, lemon juice, and spices until cooked. Simmer for additional 10 minutes and periodically deglaze the pan with a little water or additional broth to make the sauce.

HCG DIET Tip
Chop up fresh herbs and spices and freeze with water in ice cube trays. Add these as needed when cooking to flavor your dishes. Works well with fresh herbs such as basil, Italian parsley, and cilantro.

Slow Roasted Beef Brisket

Ingredients
Lean beef brisket in weighed 100 gram increments
   (example 600 grams = 6 servings)
1 ½ cups celery per serving of beef, diced
1 tablespoon garlic powder
1 tablespoon onion powder
1 tablespoon paprika
¼ cup onion, chopped
5 cloves of garlic, crushed and chopped
Cayenne pepper to taste
Chili pepper to taste
Salt and fresh ground black pepper to taste

Combine spices in a small bowl. Rub the mixture into the beef on all sides. Salt the meat liberally. Place the brisket in a crock pot. Fill about ½ ways with water. Add celery to the liquid and set crock pot on high for 30 minutes. Reduce heat to medium or low and allow to slow cook for 6-8 hours. Baste and turn the brisket periodically. You may add more of the spice mixture if you wish. Enjoy with **Horseradish Marinade/Dipping Sauce**. Save the juices, skim the fat, and use to make flavorful sauces and dressings.

Makes multiple servings
(1 protein, 1 vegetable)
21 grams protein,
9 grams fat
170 Calories

PHASE 3
MODIFICATIONS: Sear on high heat in olive oil on each side before adding to crock pot. Horseradish sauce may be modified by adding mayonnaise or Greek yogurt instead of beef broth.

Pot Roast

Ingredients
1 shoulder roast weighed in 100 gram increments
(example 900 grams = 9 servings)
1 ½ cups tomatoes per serving of beef
5 cloves garlic, chopped
½ onion, chopped
1 tablespoon paprika
Cayenne pepper to taste
Salt and black pepper to taste

Rub spices into meat on all sides. Place in crock pot and fill halfway. Add celery to liquid. Heat on high for 30 minutes then reduce heat to low and cook for 6-8 hours until fork tender. Separate into 9 equal servings and enjoy. Save the juice to make sauces and dressings. Save the celery to make soup. Always refrigerate and skim off any excess fat.

Makes multiple servings
(1 protein, 1 vegetable)
28 grams protein
8 grams fat
195 calories

PHASE 3
MODIFICATIONS: Sear on high heat with olive oil on all sides before placing in the crock-pot to cook.

Fajitas/Carne Asada

Ingredients
100 grams beef or chicken, cut into strips or flank steak asada
1 ½ cups tomatoes
1 thin slice of onion, cut into thin strips
1 clove garlic, chopped
3 tablespoons lemon juice
2 tablespoons orange juice (optional)
1/8 teaspoon oregano
1/8 teaspoon chili powder or to taste
Pinch of cayenne pepper

▶ Marinate meat in lemon juice and spices. Barbeque for carne asada or cook strips in a frying pan with garlic and onion. Add chopped tomatoes during the last 5 minutes of cooking and enjoy with lettuce leaf mock tortillas and salsa.

Makes 1 serving
(1 protein, vegetable)

23 grams protein

8 grams fat

200 calories

PHASE 3
MODIFICATIONS:
Add multi-colored bell peppers to fajitas. Use a little butter or oil for cooking. Serve with sour cream, guacamole and cheddar cheese if desired.

Meatloaf

Ingredients
100 grams ground beef (lean) for each serving
1 serving Melba toast crumbs
1 serving **Ketchup** recipe
1 tablespoon onion, chopped
1 clove garlic, minced
Cayenne pepper to taste
¼ teaspoon paprika

▶ Crush Melba toast into fine powder. Mix with the ground beef, chopped onion, and spices. Place in a baking dish, loaf pan or muffin tin for single servings. Baste with ketchup recipe mixture and bake at 350 degrees for 15-20 minutes. Cook longer for multiple servings using a loaf pan. Phase 2 variations: Use apple pulp after juicing to make meatloaf sweet and moist. Just count it as a fruit serving and enjoy the juice as an apple virgin martini or sparkling soda.

Makes 1 or more servings
(1 protein, 1 vegetable,
1 Melba toast)

20 grams protein

8 grams fat

180 calories

HCG
DIET
Tip

Add water to ground beef and simmer to reduce the fat content. As the beef cooks, the fat will float on top. Pour off the excess liquid, add spices, and enjoy. It is advisable to always choose the leanest ground beef available such as 7% or less.

Ground Beef Tacos

Ingredients
100 grams lean ground beef
Lettuce leaves
1 tablespoon onion, finely minced
1 clove garlic, crushed and minced
Dash of garlic powder
Dash of onion powder
Pinch of dried oregano
Fresh chopped cilantro to taste
Cayenne pepper to taste
Salt and black pepper to taste

Makes 1 serving
(1 protein, 1 vegetable)

20 grams protein

8 grams fat

165 calories

PHASE 3
MODIFICATIONS:
Serve with cheddar
cheese, sour cream and
guacamole.

> Brown ground beef. Add onion, garlic, and spices and a little water,
> Simmer gently for 5-10 minutes. Add salt to taste. Serve taco style in
> butter lettuce or romaine leaf mock tortillas or with a side of tomatoes
or salsa.

Veal Florentine

Ingredients
100 grams veal cutlet
1 serving Melba toast crumbs
2 cups spinach, finely chopped
¼ cup vegetable, beef broth, or water
2 tablespoons lemon juice
2 leaves of basil, rolled and sliced
1 clove garlic, crushed and minced
1 tablespoon onion, minced
Dash of garlic powder
Pinch of lemon zest
Pinch of paprika
Salt and pepper to taste

Makes 1 serving
(1 protein, 1 vegetable,
1 Melba toast)

22 grams protein

8 grams fat

198 calories

PHASE 3
MODIFICATIONS: Fry
with a little olive oil. Add
ricotta and parmesan
cheese to the spinach
mixture. Top with toasted
pine nuts and parmesan
cheese curls.

> Manually tenderize veal cutlet until flattened. Mix Melba toast crumbs
> with paprika, lemon zest, and dry spices. Then dip cutlet in lemon juice
> and spiced Melba mixture. Fry on high heat with lemon juice until
slightly browned and cooked. Remove veal cutlet from pan and deglaze
the pan with the broth. Add garlic, onion, and basil. Add spinach to the
liquid and toss lightly until slightly cooked. Top veal cutlet with spinach
mixture and spoon remaining sauce over the top. Top with salt and
pepper to taste and serve with lemon wedges.

Veal Picatta

Ingredients
100 grams veal cutlet
1 serving Melba toast crumbs
¼ cup vegetable broth or water
2 tablespoons caper juice
2 tablespoons lemon juice
1 clove of garlic, crushed and minced
Pinch of paprika
1 bay leaf
Salt and black pepper to taste

Makes 1 serving
(1 protein, 1 Melba toast)

21 grams protein

7 grams fat

165 calories

PHASE 3
MODIFICATIONS:
Deglaze the pan with ¼ cup white wine and whisk in 2 tablespoons of cold butter. Pour over veal and enjoy.

▸ Mix Melba toast crumbs with paprika, salt, and pepper. Dip veal cutlet in lemon juice and coat with herbed Melba toast crumbs. Fry veal cutlet in a little lemon juice on high heat until cooked thoroughly. Set aside cooked veal cutlet. Deglaze the pan with vegetable broth, lemon, and caper juice and add chopped garlic and bay leaf. Cook for 1-2 minutes. Remove bay leaf. Top the veal cutlet with remaining lemon sauce and garnish with lemon slices.

Veal Italian Style (try with chicken)

Ingredients
100 grams veal cutlet
1 serving Melba toast crumbs
1 serving **Marinara Sauce**
1 tablespoon onion, finely minced
1 clove of garlic, crushed and minced
¼ teaspoon dried basil
1/8 teaspoon dried oregano
Pinch of marjoram
Salt and pepper to taste

Makes 1 serving
(1 protein, 1 fruit or vegetable, 1 Melba toast)

21 grams protein

7 grams fat

235 calories

PHASE 3
MODIFICATIONS:
Top with provolone or mozzarella cheese and baste with olive oil. Enjoy with freshly grated parmesan or sautéed mushrooms.

▸ Mix Melba toast crumbs with dry spices. Dip cutlet in water or lemon juice and coat with crushed Melba spice mixture. Fry on high heat without oil. Top with marinara sauce and bake in 350 degree oven for 20 minutes. Add a little water to the bottom of the pan if necessary. Garnish with fresh basil, parsley, leftover Melba spice mixture, and salt and pepper to taste.

Mongolian Beef with Cabbage

Ingredients
100 grams sliced beef
2 cups cabbage, cut into fine strips
½ cup beef broth or water
1 tablespoon apple cider vinegar
3 tablespoons orange juice (optional)
2 tablespoons lemon juice
2 tablespoons Bragg's liquid aminos
2 cloves garlic, crushed and minced
1 tablespoon green onions, chopped
¼ teaspoon chili powder or to taste
Salt and pepper to taste
Stevia to taste

Combine spices into liquid ingredients. In frying pan or wok, stir fry on high heat to combine flavors and cook beef and cabbage. Add additional water if necessary to keep dish from burning. Add additional orange slices for added sweetness if desired.

Makes 1 serving
(1 protein, 1 vegetable)

23 grams protein

8 grams fat

205 calories

PHASE 3
MODIFICATIONS:
Stir fry with additional vegetables such as bell pepper or zucchini. Cook Mongolian Beef with sesame, chili, peanut, or coconut oil and use soy sauce to add additional flavor. Top with 1 tablespoon of crushed peanuts if desired.

Pepper Crusted Steak

Ingredients
100 grams lean steak
Fresh ground black pepper
Dash of Worcestershire sauce
Salt to taste

Manually tenderize the meat until flat. Rub meat with salt and coat liberally with black pepper. Cook on high heat for about 3-5 minutes or throw on the barbeque. Top with Worcestershire sauce, if desired, and **Caramelized Onion Garnish**. You can also cut the steak into strips and serve over a mixed green or arugula salad.

Makes 1 serving
(1 protein)

20 grams protein

7 grams fat

147 calories

PHASE 3
MODIFICATIONS: Top with blue cheese, onions, or sautéed mushrooms in butter. Or, cut into thin strips and top with onions and provolone, and make a cheese steak salad.

Beef Bourguignon

Ingredients
100 grams beef, cubed
1 cup beef broth or water
3 tablespoons tomato paste
1 tablespoon onion, chopped
1 clove garlic, crushed and sliced
Pinch of dried thyme
Pinch of marjoram
Salt & pepper to taste

Lightly braise beef cubes with onion and garlic. Combine all ingredients in small saucepan. Add liquid ingredients and spices.
Slow cook for a minimum of 30 minutes or until beef is tender. Add additional water as needed to achieve desired consistency.

Makes 1 serving
(1 protein, 1 vegetable)
21 grams protein
8 grams fat
190 calories

PHASE 3
MODIFICATIONS: Add ½ cup red wine, whisk in cold butter, and add additional non-starchy vegetables.

Hamburgers

Ingredients
100 grams lean ground hamburger (less than 7% fat)
1 tablespoon onion, finely minced
1 clove garlic, finely minced
Dash of garlic powder
Dash of onion powder
Cayenne pepper to taste
Salt and black pepper to taste

Mix ingredients thoroughly and form into patties (2-3). Fry in small frying pan until desired level of doneness or grill on the barbeque.
If using frying pan add small amounts of water and deglaze pan to intensify flavors. Cook approximately 3 minutes each side or to desired level of doneness. Variations: Add Stevia, lemon juice, and Bragg's liquid aminos to create a slight teriyaki flavor or top with **Caramelized Onion Garnish**. Also try lean buffalo or bison meat.

Makes 1 serving
(1 protein)
20 grams protein
8 grams fat
150 calories

PHASE 3
MODIFICATIONS: Add crumbled Gorgonzola cheese to the hamburger meat before cooking. Top cooked hamburgers with Swiss cheese and sautéed mushrooms or top with chili and cheese.

Gingered Beef

Ingredients
100 grams beef, cut into thin strips
¼ cup beef broth or water
1 tablespoon Bragg's liquid aminos
2 tablespoons apple cider vinegar
2 tablespoons lemon juice
1-2 tablespoons green onions, chopped
¼ teaspoon fresh ginger, grated
1 clove garlic, crushed and minced
Stevia to taste (optional)
Salt and pepper to taste

Makes 1 serving
(1 protein)

21 grams protein

8 grams fat

148 calories

> Sauté ginger and spices in broth and liquid ingredients to release the flavors. Add the beef and stir fry gently. Deglaze the pan periodically by adding a little water. Add the chopped green onions and serve hot.

Cabbage Rolls

Ingredients
100 grams lean ground beef, each serving
4 large cabbage leaves
1 cup beef broth
1 tablespoon onion, chopped
1 clove garlic, crushed and minced
Dash of garlic powder
Dash of onion powder

Makes 1 serving
(1 protein, 1 vegetable)

22 grams protein

8 grams fat

167 calories

> Preheat oven to 375 degrees. Lightly blanch large cabbage leaves and set aside. In small frying pan combine ground beef, onion, garlic, and spices and cook until brown. Spoon ground beef mixture into cabbage leaves, tuck in ends and roll up (burrito style). Put cabbage rolls in a baking dish and add broth to the bottom of the pan. Brush lightly with beef broth and bake in oven for 20-30 minutes. Spoon sauce over cabbage rolls periodically to keep moist. Make multiple servings at one time for best results.

HCG DIET Tip *Make tasty dressings and sauces from entree broths or roasting juices. Add additional spices and/or vinegar and enjoy.*

Italian Beef Roll Ups

Ingredients
100 grams lean flank steak
1 ½ cups cabbage, finely chopped
1 cup beef broth or water
2 tablespoons apple cider vinegar
1 tablespoon Bragg's liquid aminos
1 clove garlic, crushed and minced
1 tablespoon onion, minced
1 teaspoon Italian herb mix
Salt and pepper to taste

▶ Tenderize steak with manual meat tenderizer until flat and thin. In a frying pan combine cabbage with spices, vinegar, and Bragg's and cook until slightly tender. Spoon cabbage mixture onto pounded flank steak and wrap into a roll. Fill the bottom of the pan with a little water and beef broth. Salt and spice the top of the roll. Bake in 375 degree oven for approximately 20 minutes until cooked and cabbage tender. Baste occasionally with juices to keep the rolls moist. Variations: Substitute spinach for the cabbage filling.

Makes 1 serving
(1 protein, 1 vegetable)

22 grams protein

8 grams fat

205 calories

PHASE 3
MODIFICATIONS: Top with herbed cream cheese, marinara sauce, Alfredo sauce or provolone cheese and bake until bubbly and brown. Substitute chopped broccoli and cheddar cheese for the filling.

Corned Beef Hash

Ingredients
Leftover corned beef from corned beef and cabbage
Leftover cabbage, **Radish Relish** recipe, or **Marinated Apple Relish**
1 tablespoon onion, minced
1 clove garlic, crushed and minced
Pinch of fresh thyme
Pinch of fresh oregano, chopped
Salt and pepper to taste

▶ Chop up corned beef into finely diced chunks. Combine with finely chopped leftover cabbage or one serving of radish or apple relish and spices and mix well. Preheat non-stick or cast iron skillet. Press corned beef mixture into pan firmly and cover. Cook for approximately 5-6 minutes on medium heat until lightly browned. Add a little beef broth or water to deglaze, mix and press down again, cooking for an additional 5-6 minutes. Repeat as necessary until hot and lightly browned.

Makes 1 serving
(1 protein, 1 vegetable or fruit)

22 grams protein

8 grams fat

195 calories

PHASE 3
MODIFICATIONS: Use butter to cook the corned beef mixture and add bell peppers and additional vegetables if you like (make sure they are not starchy vegetables).

Baked Italian Meatballs

Ingredients
100 grams lean ground beef
¼ teaspoon basil
1/8 teaspoon oregano
1/8 teaspoon garlic powder
1/8 teaspoon oregano
1 tablespoon onion, minced
1 clove garlic, crushed and minced
1 serving Melba toast crumbs
1 serving **Marinara Sauce** recipe

▶ Combine meat, crumbs, and spices, and mix thoroughly. Form into balls. Place into baking dish and cover with marinara sauce. Bake for 20-30 minutes at 350 degrees. Garnish with fresh basil.

Makes 1 serving
(1 protein, 1 vegetable,
1 Melba toast)

21 grams protein

9 grams fat

226 calories

PHASE 3
MODIFICATIONS: Top with sliced provolone cheese or mozzarella cheese and bake until brown and bubbly. Top with grated parmesan.

Corned Beef with Cabbage

Ingredients
Beef brisket, total weight calculated in 100 gram increments
1 ½ cups cabbage per serving of beef
½ cup apple cider vinegar
½ onion, chopped
1 teaspoon powdered mustard
¼ teaspoon fresh thyme
1 bay leaf
Pinch of allspice
1 teaspoon whole black peppercorns
Liquid smoke to taste (optional)
Salt and pepper to taste

▶ Salt and pepper the beef and lightly dust with mustard. Put meat, onion and spices into a crock-pot or large pot and cover with water. Add vinegar. Bring to a boil and then reduce heat and simmer for 1 hour. Skim the fat from the water as it rises. Add the cabbage to the pot and cook for an additional 1-2 hours until the meat and cabbage are tender. Slice thinly across the grain, measure into equal servings, and serve with **Horseradish Dipping Sauce.**

Makes multiple servings
(1 protein, 1 vegetable)

22 grams protein

9 grams fat

200 calories

HCG DIET Tip *Grind your own hamburger and chicken breast using a grinder or food processor set to pulse. This allows you to control the fat content of the meat better and allows you to make entrees using ground meats without compromising the fat restrictions of the diet.*

Herbed London Broil

Ingredients
100 grams lean London broil, cut into strips
¼ cup beef broth or water
1 tablespoon onion, minced
1 clove garlic, crushed and minced
1/8 teaspoon thyme
Pinch of rosemary
Salt and pepper to taste
Italian parsley, chopped

Makes 1 serving
(1 protein)

20 grams protein

7 grams fat

155 calories

> Salt and pepper the beef strips. In a small frying pan or non-stick skillet combine London broil, herbs and beef broth. Cook until desired level of doneness. Garnish with fresh chopped parsley.

Baked Stuffed Tomatoes

Ingredients
100 grams ground beef
2 medium sized tomatoes
1 serving of Melba toast crumbs
1 tablespoon onion, finely minced
1 clove garlic, crushed and minced
1/8 teaspoon garlic powder
1/8 teaspoon onion powder
Cayenne pepper to taste
Salt and pepper to taste

Makes 1 serving
(1 protein, 1 vegetable,
1 Melba toast)

23 grams protein

9 grams fat

215 calories

> Hollow out the tomatoes, sprinkle with salt, and turn upside down to drain for 10 minutes. Brown ground beef in a small frying pan; add onion, garlic and spices. Pack ground beef mixture into tomatoes, add small amount of water to bottom of dish. Top with Melba toast crumbs and salt, and bake in 350 degree oven for 20 minutes. Garnish with fresh parsley and serve.

HCG DIET Tip *If eating organic is important to you, consider online sites for organic meats and vegetables if you have a difficult time finding them locally. Many of these companies will ship organic produce and meats to your door.*

Sloppy Joes/Barbecued Beef

Ingredients
100 grams ground beef
1 serving **Barbecue Sauce** recipe

▶ Brown ground beef in small frying pan. Add **Barbecue Sauce** and a
little water to achieve desired consistency. Cook for about 5 minutes.

Makes 1 serving
(1 protein, 1 vegetable)

21 grams protein

9 grams fat

193 calories

PHASE 3
MODIFICATIONS: Top
with cheddar cheese
slices and Stevia
caramelized onion rings.

Savory Beef Stew

Ingredients
100 grams lean steak (round, London broil, or any other lean steak), finely
cubed or whole.
1 ½ cups chopped celery per serving of beef
1 cup beef broth or water
1 tablespoon onion, chopped
1 clove garlic, crushed and minced
1/8 teaspoon onion powder
1/8 teaspoon garlic powder
Pinch of oregano
Cayenne pepper to taste
Salt and pepper to taste

Makes multiple servings
(1 protein, 1 vegetable)

22 grams protein

8 grams fat

185 calories per serving

PHASE 3
MODIFICATIONS: Add
additional non-starchy
vegetables.

▶ In saucepan, lightly brown cubed beef, onion and garlic. Add water,
vegetables, and spices and bring to a boil. Reduce heat and simmer
for approximately 30 minutes to an hour, or until the beef is tender. Add
water as needed to create a stew like consistency. Serve hot and enjoy.
Garnish with parsley. This also works as a crock pot recipe. Just add
additional water and slow cook whole 100 gram servings instead of cubed.

NOTE: This is a slow cooked dish so, for multiple servings, weigh out in
hundred gram increments and then divide into equal servings at the end
of the cooking process.

Roasted Beef and Apple Kabobs

Ingredients
100 grams of lean good quality beef or chunked chicken
1 apple, cut into large chunks
¼ onion petals
½ cup beef, chicken, or vegetable broth
2 tablespoons apple cider vinegar
1 tablespoon Bragg's liquid aminos
Stevia to taste

Makes 1 serving
(1 protein, 1 fruit)

21 grams protein

8 grams fat

240 calories

Marinate beef or chicken in broth, vinegar, and spices. Layer apple, onion petals, and beef or protein chunks on wooden or metal skewers (if using wooden skewers soak them for a few minutes so they don't burn). Place directly on barbecue or on aluminum foil sheet and cook until desired level of doneness. Baste frequently with remaining marinade. Heat the remaining marinade in a small sauce pan and use as a dipping sauce.

Stuffed Chard Rolls

Ingredients
100 grams lean ground beef (per serving)
1 or more large chard leaves, any kind
1 cup beef broth
1 tablespoon onion, finely minced
1 clove of garlic, crushed and minced
1/8 teaspoon basil
1/8 teaspoon oregano
1/8 teaspoon onion powder
1/8 teaspoon garlic powder
Cayenne pepper to taste
Salt and pepper to taste

Makes 1 serving
(1 protein, 1 vegetable)

22 grams protein

9 grams fat

175 calories (add 50 more calories if using marinara sauce)

Cook ground beef with a little water. Add spices, garlic, and onion to the beef. Lightly steam chard leaves until slightly soft. Wrap ground beef in chard leaf burrito style. Place wraps in baking dish. Cover with beef broth and bake at 350 degrees for 20 minutes. Garnish with fresh spices or parsley.

HCG DIET Tip *Look for items at a good price in bulk and freeze what you can't use immediately.*

Curried Shrimp with Tomatoes

Ingredients
100 grams shrimp
½ cup vegetable broth or water
1 ½ cups tomatoes, chopped
1 tablespoon onion, minced
1 clove garlic, crushed and minced
1/8 teaspoon curry or to taste
1/8 teaspoon onion powder
1/8 teaspoon garlic powder
Pinch of allspice
Stevia to taste

Makes 1 serving
(1 protein, 1 vegetable)
20 grams protein
1.5 grams fat
165 calories

Sauté the shrimp with the onion and garlic for about 3 minutes or until cooked. Add vegetable broth, curry and Stevia. Add garlic and onion powder to thicken the mixture. Cook for 5-10 minutes on medium heat. Add water or reduce liquid until desired consistency is reached.

Shrimp Etouffee

Ingredients
100 grams shrimp
½ cup vegetable broth or water
1 ½ cups celery, chopped
1 clove garlic, crushed and minced
1 tablespoon red onion, chopped
1 tablespoon green onion, chopped
Pinch of thyme
Pinch of cayenne pepper to taste
Salt and pepper to taste

Makes 1 serving
(1 protein, 1 vegetable)
21 grams protein
2 grams fat
135 calories

PHASE 3
MODIFICATIONS: Start sauce with browned butter. Add a splash of dry sherry to the sauce and whisk in additional cold chunks of butter to create a richer more flavorful sauce.

Add spices and vegetables to broth and simmer for about 15 minutes until celery is softened. Add the shrimp to the mixture and cook an additional 10-20 minutes. Serve hot.

Creole Shrimp

Ingredients
100 grams shrimp
½ cup vegetable broth or water
1 clove garlic, crushed and minced
1 tablespoon onion, minced
¼ teaspoon horseradish
1/8 teaspoon garlic powder
1/8 teaspoon onion powder
1-2 teaspoons hot sauce
2 tablespoons lemon juice
Pinch of thyme
1 bay leaf
Dash of sassafras powder or root beer flavored Stevia
Dash of liquid smoke flavoring (optional)
Cayenne pepper to taste
Salt and black pepper to taste

Makes 1 serving (1 protein)	
20 grams protein	
1.5 grams fat	
115 calories	

Mix liquid ingredients, onion, garlic, and spices. Simmer over low heat for 10 minutes in a small frying pan. Add shrimp and cook thoroughly for an additional 5 minutes. Add salt and pepper to taste. Deglaze the pan periodically with additional water or broth. Serve hot or cold over a salad or with fresh asparagus.

Shrimp Scampi

Ingredients
100 grams shrimp
¼ cup vegetable broth or water
3 tablespoons lemon juice
4 cloves garlic, crushed and minced
Dash of garlic powder
Dash of onion powder
Dash of chili or cayenne pepper powder to taste
Salt and pepper to taste

Makes 1 serving (1 protein)	
20 grams protein	
1.5 grams fat	
115 calories	

Add garlic to liquid ingredients. Add shrimp and additional spices. Cook for 5-7 minutes until shrimp are pink and liquid is reduced. Serve hot or cold with a salad or on a bed of spinach.

Sweet Ginger Shrimp

Ingredients
100 grams shrimp
¼ cup vegetable broth or water
2 tablespoons lemon juice
2 tablespoons orange juice (optional)
1 tablespoon Bragg's liquid aminos
¼ teaspoon ginger, fresh or powdered
Pinch of chili powder
Dash of garlic powder
Dash of onion powder
Stevia to taste
Salt and black pepper to taste

Makes 1 serving
(1 protein)

20 grams protein

1.5 grams fat

125 calories

▶ Mix dry spices with vegetable broth and liquid ingredients. Sauté with shrimp in small saucepan stirring continuously until cooked. Add water to deglaze the pan periodically until desired consistency is reached.

Black Pepper Sautéed Shrimp

Ingredients
100 grams shrimp
1 serving Melba toast crumbs (optional)
2 tablespoons lemon juice
1 tablespoon caper juice
Salt and fresh ground black pepper to taste

Makes 1 serving
(1 protein, 1 Melba toast)

20 grams protein

1.5 grams fat

120 calories

▶ Mix Melba toast crumbs with salt and generous amount of black pepper. Coat shrimp with Melba toast/pepper mixture and fry on high heat in a skillet in a little lemon juice until cooked well. Serve hot and garnish with lemon and additional freshly ground black pepper.

Jambalaya

Ingredients
100 grams shrimp (chicken, beef, or **Chicken Sausage** can be used)
1 ½ cups tomatoes or celery, chopped (tomatoes add an additional 25 calories)
1 cup vegetable broth or water
1 tablespoon lemon juice
1 tablespoon onion, chopped
1 clove garlic, crushed and minced
Dash of Worcestershire sauce
Dash of hot sauce
Dash of liquid smoke (optional)
Pinch of cayenne to taste
1/8 teaspoon garlic powder
1/8 teaspoon onion powder
Pinch of thyme
Salt and pepper
Water as needed

Makes 1 serving
(1 protein, 1 vegetable, 1 fruit)

21 grams protein

2 grams fat

150 calories

PHASE 3
MODIFICATIONS:
Add chopped red and green bell pepper and additional seafood, chicken, sausage, etc.

Lightly sauté shrimp or chicken with celery or tomatoes, garlic and onion in lemon juice until cooked or lightly browned. Deglaze the pan with broth and add seasonings. Simmer on low for approximately 20-30 minutes until liquid is slightly reduced adding additional broth or water to achieve desired consistency.

H C G
D I E T
Tip *Cook a roast in advance. Weigh the whole roast in 100 gram raw increments, then divide the roast into individual servings at the end of the cooking process.*

Ginger Shrimp Wraps

Ingredients
100 grams shrimp
1 or more cabbage or lettuce leaves
1 cup vegetable broth or water
2 teaspoons apple cider vinegar
1 tablespoon Bragg's liquid aminos
1 clove garlic, crushed and minced
Pinch of fresh ginger
1 tablespoon green onion, finely minced
1 serving **Spicy Orange Sauce** (optional, for dipping)
Salt and pepper to taste

Makes 1 serving
(1 protein, 1 vegetable)

20 grams protein

2 grams fat

165 calories

PHASE 3
MODIFICATIONS: Add a
drizzle of sesame, peanut
or hot chili oil to the
shrimp mixture for added
flavor.

▶ Lightly steam cabbage leaves and then set aside. Cook shrimp with spices and mince together with onion. Wrap up shrimp mixture in cabbage or lettuce leaves and enjoy with dipping sauce. Another alternative is to place multiple rolls in small baking dish. Cover with vegetable broth and bake for 25 minutes at 350 degrees. Variations: Dip wraps in **Sweet Wasabi Dipping Sauce** or top with additional Bragg's.

Baked Curried Fish

Ingredients
100 grams white fish
2 tablespoons lemon juice
1 serving Melba toast crumbs
1 tablespoon onion, finely chopped
1 clove garlic, crushed and minced
1/8 teaspoon onion powder
1/8 teaspoon garlic powder
1/8 teaspoon curry powder
Salt and pepper to taste
Fresh parsley

Makes 1 serving
(1 protein, 1 Melba toast)

20 grams protein

5 grams fat

137 calories

▶ Combine dry spices and Melba toast crumbs. Dip fish into Melba and spice mixture to coat thoroughly. Broil fish until fish is cooked and herbed crumb mixture is slightly brown. Garnish with lemon slices and fresh parsley.

Tilapia with Herbs

Ingredients
100 grams of Tilapia fish (Substitute any white fish)
2 tablespoons lemon juice
1 clove garlic, crushed and minced
1 tablespoon onion, chopped
Pinch of dill
Fresh parsley
Salt and black pepper to taste

Makes 1 serving
(1 protein)

20 grams protein

1.5 grams fat

115 calories

▶ Sauté fish in lemon juice with a little water, then add onion, garlic, and fresh herbs. Garnish with chopped parsley. Or bake in baking dish with a little water at 350 degrees for 20 minutes until fish is tender and delicious.

Variations: oregano, thyme, or tarragon.

Poached White Fish

Ingredients
100 grams per serving white fish
½ cup vegetable broth or water
1 tablespoon lemon juice
1 tablespoon onion, chopped
1 clove garlic, crushed and minced
½ teaspoon fresh ginger
Pinch of grated orange zest
Salt and pepper to taste
Stevia to taste

Makes one serving
(1 protein)

20 grams protein

4 grams fat

137 calories

▶ Heat up the vegetable broth in small frying pan. Add lemon juice, onion, garlic, and spices. Poach white fish filet for 5-10 minutes until fish is tender and cooked thoroughly. May also be wrapped in foil and placed on the barbeque. Serve topped with remaining juices as a sauce.

HCG DIET *Tip* *Substitute any variety of low fat fresh white fish in any of the fish recipes in this book so you can make choices that are convenient for you and seasonally available.*

Crab Cakes

Ingredients
100 grams snow or king crab meat
1 serving Melba toast crumbs
1 tablespoon lemon juice
1 teaspoon apple cider vinegar
1/8 teaspoon onion powder
1/8 teaspoon garlic powder
1 tablespoon onion, finely minced
1 clove garlic, crushed and minced
Cayenne pepper to taste
Salt and black pepper to taste

Makes 1 serving
(1 protein, 1 Melba toast)
20 grams protein
1 gram fat
125 calories

PHASE 3
MODIFICATIONS: Add
a little egg to the crab
mixture and fry with a
little butter or oil. Serve
with Cajun spiced cream
sauce or mayonnaise.

> In a small bowl combine ingredients and form into cakes. Press crab
> cakes into muffin tins and bake at 350 degrees for about 10-20 minutes
> until slightly brown on top. The crab mixture can also be sautéed until
warm or chilled and served over a green salad with lemon garnish and
topped with Melba toast crumbs.

Cajun Baked Fish

Ingredients
100 grams of white fish
1 serving Melba toast crumbs
1/8 teaspoon onion powder
1/8 teaspoon garlic powder
Pinch of cayenne pepper to taste
Pinch of thyme
Salt and black pepper to taste

Makes 1 serving
(1 protein, 1 Melba toast)
20 grams protein
4 grams fat
120 calories

PHASE 3
MODIFICATIONS: Dip
fish in egg and brush with
olive oil. Serve with a
Cajun cream sauce.

> Combine spices and Melba toast powder. Dip fish in lemon juice and
> coat with spice mixture. Bake in 350 degree oven for 20 minutes or
> broil until lightly brown. Garnish with parsley.

Lemon Dill Fish

100 grams, any kind of white fish
4 tablespoons lemon juice
¼ cup vegetable broth or water
1 teaspoon apple cider vinegar
1 teaspoon fresh dill
1 clove garlic, crushed and minced
1 tablespoon onion, minced
Salt and black pepper to taste

Makes 1 serving
(1 protein)

20 grams protein

3 grams fat

110 calories

▶ Sauté fish with lemon juice, vegetable broth, and vinegar. Add garlic, onion, and fresh dill. Cook for an additional 5-10 minutes or until fish is completely cooked. Garnish with lemon wedges.

Italian Shrimp with Tomatoes

Ingredients
100 grams shrimp
1 ½ cups tomatoes, chopped
¼ cup vegetable broth or water
2 tablespoons lemon juice
¼ teaspoon basil, dried or fresh
2 cloves of garlic, crushed and minced
Pinch of dried or fresh oregano
Pinch of red pepper flakes
Salt and black pepper to taste

Makes 1 serving
(1 protein, 1 vegetable)

20 grams protein

1.5 grams fat

160 calories

PHASE 3
MODIFICATIONS: Sauté with a little olive oil. Add chopped zucchini or other vegetables. Top with fresh grated parmesan cheese.

▶ Sauté onion, garlic and spices in broth and lemon juice. Add spices and cook for 5 minutes. Add the shrimp and tomatoes and cook until shrimp is pink and well cooked.

Sweet Wasabi Sautéed Shrimp

Ingredients
100 grams shrimp
1 recipe **Sweet Wasabi Marinade**
1 tablespoon onion, minced
Pinch of ginger, dried or fresh Stevia to taste

Makes 1 serving (1 protein)
20 grams protein
1.5 grams fat
110 calories

▸ Sauté shrimp with onion in wasabi marinade. Serve hot or enjoy chilled over mixed green salad.

Spicy Mustard Shrimp with Chard

Ingredients
100 grams shrimp
1 ½ cups chard, chopped
½ cup vegetable broth or water
3 tablespoons **Homemade Mustard**
1 tablespoon Bragg's liquid aminos
1 tablespoon apple cider vinegar
2 tablespoons lemon juice
Pinch of red pepper flakes
2 tablespoons onion, chopped
2 cloves garlic, sliced
Salt and pepper to taste

Makes 1 serving (1 protein, 1 vegetable)
21 grams protein
1.5 grams fat
145 calories

PHASE 3
MODIFICATIONS: Cook with a little olive oil, sesame oil or walnut oil. Top with 2 tablespoons chopped roasted almonds.

▸ Sauté the shrimp with onion, garlic, Bragg's, vinegar, lemon juice, and mustard until cooked. Remove the shrimp and deglaze the pan with the vegetable broth. Add chard to the broth and cook, stirring occasionally until chard is tender. Add a little water if needed. Top with mustard shrimp and enjoy.

Baked White Fish with Asparagus

Ingredients
100 grams white fish (make multiple servings for best results)
1 ½ cups asparagus per serving of fish
1 serving Melba toast crumbs per serving
½ cup vegetable broth or water
2 tablespoons caper juice
4 tablespoons lemon juice
1 clove garlic, crushed and minced
1 tablespoon onion, minced
¼ teaspoon dill, dried or fresh
Pinch of tarragon
Parsley
Salt and pepper to taste

Makes 1 serving
(1 protein, 1 vegetable,
1 Melba toast)

21 grams protein

4 grams fat

215 calories

In a small baking dish, layer the fish and asparagus. Mix vegetable broth with spices and pour over fish and asparagus. Top with herbed Melba toast crumbs and bake at 350 degrees for about 20 minutes or until fish and asparagus are cooked thoroughly and crumbs are slightly brown. Top with remaining sauce, fresh parsley, and serve with lemon wedges. Dish can also be cooked on the barbecue. Just wrap up fish and asparagus in foil, toss with spices, and baste with vegetable broth.

Poached Fish with Thyme

Ingredients
100 grams white fish
½ cup vegetable broth or water
2 tablespoons caper juice
2 tablespoons lemon juice
1 teaspoon apple cider vinegar
1 clove garlic, crushed and minced
1 tablespoon red onion, minced
1/8 teaspoon thyme
Salt and pepper to taste

Makes 1 serving
(1 protein)

20 grams protein

2 grams fat

140 calories

PHASE 3
MODIFICATIONS: Brush
fish with melted butter
or olive oil. Top with a
tablespoon of capers.

Add garlic, onion, and spices to liquid ingredients. Add fish and poach for 5 minutes or until fish is cooked thoroughly. Garnish with parsley and lemon.

Orange or Lemon Glazed Orange Roughy BBQ Wrap

Ingredients
100 grams orange roughy fish
3 orange slices
3 tablespoons orange juice (optional)
1 tablespoon lemon juice
1 tablespoon green onion, minced
Dash of garlic powder
Dash of onion powder
Salt and pepper to taste
Stevia to taste

Makes 1 serving
(1 protein, 1 fruit)
16 grams protein
1 gram fat
115 calories 115

> Place fish on aluminum foil. Baste with juice and spices. Top with orange or lemon slices. Wrap up and place on barbeque or in the stove at 350 degrees for 10-15 minutes until well cooked and fork tender. Serve with juices and orange slices. Sprinkle with parsley.

Sweet Orange Pepper Shrimp

Ingredients
100 grams shrimp
1 tablespoon onion, minced
1 serving of **Sweet Orange Marinade**
Few slices of orange, chopped
Black pepper to taste
Stevia to taste

Makes 1 serving
(1 protein, 1 fruit)
20 grams protein
2 grams fat
125 calories

> Marinate shrimp for 30 minutes in marinade. In small frying pan add shrimp and rest of marinade along with a few chopped slices of orange. Add black pepper to taste. Deglaze the pan periodically with water, Sauté until shrimp are cooked and tender and the sauce is the right consistency.

HCG DIET Tip *Crush one serving of Melba toast, mix with herbs, and use as a topping for baked fish or chicken.*

Lobster Medallions in Tomato Sauce

Ingredients
100 grams raw lobster tail
1 ½ cups tomatoes, chopped
2 ounces tomato sauce
2 tablespoons lemon juice
1 clove of garlic, crushed and minced
1 tablespoon onion, minced
1 bay leaf
1/8 teaspoon thyme
1/8 teaspoon fresh tarragon, chopped
Cayenne pepper to taste
Salt and pepper to taste
Chopped parsley
Salt and fresh ground black pepper to taste

Makes 1 serving
(1 protein, 1 vegetable)

23 grams protein

2 grams fat

175 calories

PHASE 3
MODIFICATIONS: Add
a drizzle of olive oil or
add small cubes of cold
unsalted butter and stir in
quickly for a richer sauce.
Add a splash of white
wine or dry sherry and
a tablespoon of heavy
cream.

Slice medallions of lobster tail. Weigh out 100 grams raw. Sauté lobster in lemon juice and a little water then add garlic, onion, tomatoes, tomato sauce, and spices. Simmer for 10-15 minutes and serve.

Baked Stuffed Lobster

Ingredients
100 grams raw lobster tail
1 serving Melba toast crumbs
½ cup vegetable broth or water
1 tablespoon onion, minced
1 clove garlic, crushed and minced
1/8 teaspoon garlic powder
1/8 teaspoon onion powder
Paprika to taste
Salt and pepper to taste

Makes 1 serving
(1 protein, 1 Melba toast)

20 grams protein

1 gram fat

115 calories

PHASE 3
MODIFICATIONS: Add
parmesan cheese to the
stuffing and serve with
melted butter.

Mix Melba toast crumbs with spices, garlic, and onion. Stuff lobster tail with Melba mixture and place into baking dish, stuffing side up. Pour vegetable broth over the lobster, dust the lobster with more paprika and bake at 350 degrees for approximately 20 minutes. Broil for an additional 1-2 minutes to brown. Add salt and pepper to taste and serve with lemon wedges.

Savory Onion Caramelized Shrimp

Ingredients
100 grams shrimp
Sliced onion cut into rings (whole onion is counted as a vegetable)
¼ cup water
3 tablespoons lemon juice
1 tablespoon Bragg's liquid aminos
Vanilla flavored liquid Stevia to taste
Salt and pepper to taste

> Heat up the liquid ingredients on high heat in small frying pan. Add Stevia, salt, pepper, onion, and shrimp. Deglaze with a little water several times to create a caramelized sauce.

Makes 1 serving
(1 protein, 1 vegetable)

22 grams protein

1.5 grams fat

200 calories

Sweet and Sour Shrimp

Ingredients
100 grams shrimp
1 cup water
½ lemon with rind
½ orange with rind
2 tablespoons Bragg's liquid aminos
1 tablespoon onion, minced
1 clove garlic, crushed and minced
Cayenne pepper to taste
Salt and pepper to taste
Stevia to taste

> Boil 1 cup of water with ½ lemon and ½ orange with rind until pulp comes out of the center. Scrape out remaining pulp and discard the rind. Add onion, garlic, Bragg's, and spices and reduce liquid by half. Add the shrimp to the sauce and sauté for 5-7 minutes until shrimp is cooked.

Makes 1 serving
(1 protein, 1 fruit)

20 grams protein

2 grams fat

110 calories

PHASE 3
MODIFICATIONS: Add red and green bell peppers to the mix. Add sesame or chili oil to the recipe and a small amount of fresh pineapple. (Pineapple should be used sparingly due to the high sugar content)

Shrimp with Mint and Cilantro

Ingredients
100 grams shrimp
2 tablespoons fresh cilantro, finely minced
1 tablespoon fresh mint, finely minced
1 teaspoon fresh Italian parsley
1 clove garlic, crushed and minced
2 tablespoons lemon juice
Salt and pepper to taste
Stevia (optional)

> In a small frying pan, fry up the garlic in the lemon juice. Add shrimp, cilantro, mint and parsley. Stir fry together until shrimp is cooked and coated with herb mixture. Add a little extra water or lemon juice if necessary. Garnish with lemon wedges.

Makes 1 serving
(1 protein)

20 grams protein

1.5 grams fat

105 calories

PHASE 3
MODIFICATIONS: Add a little olive oil and parmesan cheese, and top with walnuts or pine nuts.

Orange Roughy with Tomatoes and Onion

Ingredients
100 grams orange roughy fish
1 ½ cups tomatoes, chopped
2 tablespoons onion, minced
1 clove garlic, crushed and minced
½ cup vegetable broth or water
Salt and pepper to taste

> Sauté onions and garlic in vegetable broth. Add orange roughy and spices until almost cooked about 5 minutes. Add freshly chopped tomatoes and cook for an additional 5 minutes. Serve hot, add salt and pepper to taste. Garnish with parsley.

Makes 1 serving
(1 protein, 1 vegetable)

22 grams protein

2 grams fat

160 calories

PHASE 3
MODIFICATIONS: Sauté onions and garlic in butter. Add ¼ cup half and half.

Sautéed Snapper with Lemon Pepper Sauce

Ingredients
100 grams red snapper
¼ cup vegetable broth or water
2 tablespoons lemon juice
2 tablespoons caper juice
Dash of garlic powder
Dash of onion powder
Dash of cayenne (optional)
Salt and fresh ground pepper to taste

Add dry spices to broth and liquid ingredients. Sauté fish in sauce for 5-10 minutes until thoroughly cooked.

Makes 1 serving
(1 protein)

20 grams protein	
1.5 grams fat	
110 calories	

PHASE 3 MODIFICATIONS: Whisk in small cubes of unsalted butter to create a lemon butter sauce.

Blackened Red Snapper

Ingredients
100 grams red snapper fish

Blackening Spice Mix
Ingredients
2 teaspoons paprika
4 teaspoons thyme
2 teaspoons onion powder
2 teaspoons garlic powder
1 teaspoon cayenne pepper
2 teaspoons oregano
½ teaspoon cumin
½ teaspoon nutmeg powder
2 teaspoons salt
2 teaspoons black pepper
Stevia

Makes 1 serving
(1 protein)

20 grams protein	
2 grams fat	
110 calories	

Mix spices well in shaker jar. On a paper plate remove enough of the spice mixture to coat pieces of fish thoroughly. Preheat a skillet to high heat. Add fish dry and cook quickly until spices are blackened and fish is cooked completely. Serve hot. Garnish with lemon and fresh parsley. Save the rest of the blackened spice mixture to use later. Works well with chicken also.

HCG DIET Tip *Many of the seafood recipes in this cookbook can also be modified to taste delicious with chicken or beef.*

Baked Lobster with Spicy Lemon Sauce

Ingredients
100 grams sliced lobster tail
1 serving Melba toast crumbs
¼ cup water
4 tablespoons lemon juice
Pinch of red pepper flakes
¼ teaspoon garlic powder
Pinch of sweet paprika
Pinch of lemon zest
1 teaspoon fresh parsley, chopped
Salt and pepper to taste

Makes 1 serving
(1 protein, 1 Melba toast)

20 grams protein

2 grams fat

110 calories

> In a small saucepan combine water and lemon juice with spices and
> bring to a boil. Reduce liquid and deglaze occasionally. Lay out slices
of lobster in small baking dish. Pour lemon sauce over lobster and
sprinkle with Melba crumbs, paprika, salt, and fresh ground pepper. Bake
lobster slices at 350 degrees for approximately 15 minutes or until lobster
is fully cooked. Add a little extra water if needed so lobster doesn't burn.
Serve hot and topped with sauce. Garnish with lemon slices and sprinkle
with lemon zest and parsley.

Citrus Fish

Ingredients
100 grams white fish
1 tablespoon onion, minced
2 tablespoons lemon juice
Lemon and orange zest to taste
Lemon and orange slices
Chopped parsley
Salt and pepper to taste
Stevia to taste

Makes one serving
(1 protein, 1 fruit)

20 grams protein

2 grams fat

110 calories

> Mix lemon juice with zest and a little Stevia. Baste fish with mixture
> and top with salt, pepper, and lemon and orange slices. Wrap in
aluminum foil and place on the barbeque or in oven at 350 degrees.
Cook fish for 5-10 minutes or until fish is thoroughly cooked. Serve with
lemon and top with parsley.

Mahi Mahi with Oranges

Ingredients
100 grams mahi mahi fish
½ orange in segments
1 tablespoon Bragg's amino acids
1 teaspoon apple cider vinegar
1/8 teaspoon ginger, fresh or powdered
1 tablespoon green onion, chopped
1 clove garlic, crushed and minced
Pinch of red pepper flakes
Stevia to taste
Cayenne to taste
A little water as needed

Makes 1 serving
(1 protein, 1 fruit)

20 grams protein

2 grams fat

140 calories

Sauté mahi mahi fish with a little water, vinegar, and Bragg's. Add garlic, spices, and Stevia. Add ½ orange in chunks or segments. Cook for 5-10 minutes. Top with green onion and serve on a bed of steamed spinach or greens.

HCG DIET Tip
Prepare several servings of the recipes at the same time for future meals. This works especially well with baked dishes like cabbage rolls or baked fish recipes. Just adjust the sauces and spices for individual servings as necessary.

Cabbage Rice/Noodle Alternative

Ingredients
½ - 1 head of cabbage, finely chopped into rice size or noodle size pieces
Your choice of spices
1 cup chicken, vegetable broth or water

Mexican rice style
1 cup chicken or vegetable broth
2 tablespoons onion, minced
1 clove of garlic, crushed and minced
¼ teaspoon Mexican oregano
¼ teaspoon cayenne pepper to taste
Dash of cumin to taste
Fresh chopped cilantro
Salt and pepper to taste

Italian style
1 cup chicken or vegetable broth
¼ teaspoon fresh or dried oregano
¼ teaspoon dried basil or 5 leaves fresh basil rolled and sliced
2 tablespoons onion, minced
1 clove garlic, crushed and minced
Salt and pepper to taste

Indian style
½ teaspoon curry
2 tablespoons onion, minced
1 clove garlic, crushed and minced
¼ teaspoon cumin
Salt and pepper to taste

Oriental style
½ teaspoon ginger
2 tablespoons Bragg's liquid aminos
2 tablespoons lemon juice
3 tablespoons orange juice (optional)
2 tablespoons onion, chopped
1 clove garlic, crushed and minced

In a large frying pan sauté cabbage with a little water (vegetable or chicken broth may be substituted) and liquid ingredients. Add spices and cook until cabbage is tender, adding water as necessary. Add ground beef or chicken to the spiced cabbage if desired.

Makes 2 servings
(1 vegetable)

3 grams protein

0 fat

90 calories per serving

HCG DIET Tip *Eat moderate amounts of vegetables. Dr. Simeons is fairly precise about most of the food choices for the HCG Diet except for the quantity of vegetable servings. Feel free to have more or less vegetables than the recipes in this cookbook as long as you don't go above 500 calories for the day. It may be helpful for some people to have the option to eat a few more vegetables if you are experiencing hunger.*

Garlic and Onion Spiced Chard

Ingredients
4-6 cups Swiss or red chard
1 tablespoon apple cider vinegar
½ cup vegetable, chicken broth or water
4 tablespoons lemon juice to taste
6 cloves of garlic, chopped
2 tablespoons onion, chopped
½ teaspoon garlic powder
Salt and pepper to taste

Makes 2 servings
(1 vegetable)
2 grams protein
0 fat
30 calories per serving

▶ In a frying pan add chard, water, onion, garlic, and spices to water and liquid ingredients and sauté for 5 minutes or to desired level of doneness. Sprinkle with lemon and salt and pepper to taste.

Cold Chicory Salad

Ingredients
1 cup fresh chicory, chopped
2 teaspoons apple cider vinegar
1 tablespoon Bragg's liquid aminos
1 tablespoon lemon juice
Salt and pepper to taste

Makes 1 serving
(1 vegetable)
0 protein
0 fat
20 calories

PHASE 3
MODIFICATIONS: Add
a little olive, walnut, or
hazelnut oil. Sprinkle with
1 tablespoon chopped
walnuts and feta cheese.

▶ Chop chicory very fine. Stir in apple cider vinegar and lemon juice. Add salt and fresh ground black pepper to taste. Enjoy as a side dish or cool salad. Phase 2 variations: Add tomatoes and chopped fresh mint or mix in a little orange juice. Add finely minced red onion and garlic or chopped apple and Stevia.

Caramelized Onion Garnish

Ingredients
½ large onion, cut into fine rings
4 tablespoons lemon juice
Vanilla Stevia to taste
Small amount of water as needed
Pinch of salt

Makes 4 servings
.5 grams protein
0 fat
50 calories

▶ Preheat skillet. Add small amount of water to bottom of pan and add lemon juice and Stevia. Add onion rings and cook quickly periodically deglazing the pan with a little more water to create a sweet caramel sauce. Serve immediately over steak or chicken. Spoon any remaining sauce created by deglazing over the top. Can be served chilled and added as a topping to salads.

Savory Baked Red Onion Garnish

Ingredients
½ red onion, cut into rings
¼ cup apple cider vinegar
2 tablespoons lemon juice
1 bay leaf or pinch of bay leaf powder
1 clove garlic, crushed and minced
Pinch of dried basil and oregano (optional)
Salt and pepper to taste
Small amount of water

Makes 4 servings
.5 grams protein
0 fat
50 calories

PHASE 3 MODIFICATIONS: Brush with olive oil before baking or sauté with browned butter and spices. Top with fresh grated parmesan or Romano cheese. Try baked, topped with a slice of provolone or mozzarella cheese.

▶ Put onion in a baking dish with apple cider vinegar, water, and spices. Bake at 375 degrees for 10 minutes. Serve hot over beef or chicken or chill and add to salads. Can also be sautéed in a small frying pan, deglazing periodically.

Phase 2 variations: Substitute a sprinkle of rosemary, tarragon or dill instead of other spices. Or sprinkle with poultry seasoning.

Garlic Spinach

Ingredients
1 ½ cups spinach
½ cup chicken broth or water
2 tablespoons lemon juice
2 tablespoons onion, minced
2 cloves garlic, crushed and minced
¼ teaspoon onion powder
Pinch red pepper flakes

Makes 1-2 servings
(1 vegetable)
2 grams protein
0 fat
35 calories

▶ Sauté the onion and garlic lightly in frying pan with a little water and lemon juice until soft. Add fresh garlic and spices. Stir in fresh spinach leaves and cook lightly. Serve with your favorite chicken or fish dish.

Saffron Cabbage

Ingredients
1 ½ cups cabbage, chopped
1 cup chicken broth or water
2 tablespoons onion, finely chopped
1 clove garlic, crushed and minced
Pinch of saffron powder or threads softened in water and made into a paste.
1/8 teaspoon turmeric
Dash of mustard powder
Salt and pepper to taste

Makes 1-2 servings
(1 vegetable)
1.5 grams protein
0 fat
60 calories

▶ In a large frying pan, heat chicken broth and spices. Add cabbage and cover pan with a lid. Cook cabbage until tender, adding water if necessary to keep from burning and coating with the spice mixture. Serve hot with chicken or chilled for a cool salad.

HCG DIET *Tip* *Take a weekly shopping trip to pick up wonderful, fresh, or organic produce at your local farmers market or co-op. If you go to your local grocery store, try to buy your veggies as fresh as possible for optimum nutritional value.*

Radish Relish

Ingredients
8 large red radishes
3 tablespoons of apple cider vinegar
Dash of garlic powder
Dash of onion powder
Salt and pepper to taste
Stevia to taste (optional)

Makes 1-2 servings
(1 vegetable)

1 gram protein

0 fat

20 calories

> Combine liquid ingredients with powdered spices. Finely dice radishes and marinate in liquid mixture for 1-3 hours or overnight. Use as a topping on your protein servings or as a side dish.

Indian Spiced Spinach

Ingredients
1 ½ cups spinach
2 tablespoons onion, minced
¼ cup chicken broth or water
1/8 teaspoon cumin
1/8 teaspoon paprika
1/8 teaspoon turmeric
Pinch of fresh grated ginger
Pinch of ground coriander
Salt and pepper to taste

Makes 1-2 servings
(1 vegetable)

2 grams protein

0 fat

35 calories

PHASE 3
MODIFICATIONS: Add melted butter or ghee. Stir in chunks of paneer cheese to make palak paneer, a traditional Indian dish.

> Sauté spices in chicken broth with onion. Add spinach and stir gently until cooked. (substitute ¼ teaspoon garam masala for dry spices).

Variations: Add chicken or shrimp.

Baked Celery

Ingredients
1 ½ cups celery
½ cup beef, chicken broth, or water
2 tablespoons lemon juice
1 tablespoon Bragg's liquid aminos
2 tablespoons onions, chopped
1 clove fresh garlic, chopped
1 bay leaf
Pinch of red pepper flakes
Paprika to taste
Salt and pepper to taste

Makes 1-2 servings
(1 vegetable)

2 grams protein

0 fat

38 calories

▶ Chop up celery into sticks and arrange in a baking dish. Dissolve spices in liquid ingredients and pour over the celery. Bake in 375 degree oven in until soft and lightly brown on top. Serve with the juices and sprinkle with paprika. Add salt and pepper to taste.

Chilled Tomato Salad

Ingredients
1 ½ cups tomatoes, chopped
¼ cup apple cider vinegar
1 tablespoon green onion, sliced
1 garlic clove, crushed and minced
Dash of mustard powder
¼ teaspoon basil
1/8 teaspoon thyme
1/8 teaspoon marjoram
Salt and pepper to taste

Makes 2 servings
(1 vegetable)

3 grams protein

0 fat

60 calories

PHASE 3
MODIFICATIONS: Add olive oil or mayonnaise, mix in small slices of Swiss or crumbled feta cheese and sliced green olives.

▶ Combine apple cider vinegar with spices. Pour over tomato chunks or slices. Marinate and chill for 1 hour before serving.

Pickled Beet Greens (substitute spinach)

Ingredients
1 ½ cups beet greens
¼ cup apple cider vinegar
1 tablespoon lemon juice
2 teaspoons Bragg's amino acids
1 clove garlic, crushed and sliced
2 tablespoons onion, minced
¼ teaspoon red pepper flakes or to taste
Salt and pepper to taste
Stevia to taste (optional)

Makes 1 or more servings
(1 vegetable)

2 grams protein

0 fat

30 calories

PHASE 3
MODIFICATIONS: Add 2
tablespoons of crumbled
bacon to the greens for
added flavor.

▶ Combine liquid ingredients and spices. Pour over beet greens and cook for 5-10 minutes, stirring occasionally to mix spices. Add water as necessary. Serve hot or cold.

Grilled Asparagus with Rosemary Lemon Sauce

Ingredients
1 ½ cups asparagus (approximately 5 spears)
Juice of ½ lemon with rind
1 tablespoon Bragg's liquid aminos
1 clove garlic, crushed and minced
¼ teaspoon rosemary
Dash of garlic powder
Dash of onion powder
Cayenne pepper to taste
Salt and pepper to taste

Makes 1 serving
(1 vegetable)

5 grams protein

0 fat

65 calories

▶ Marinate asparagus in lemon, garlic, salt, cayenne pepper, and Braggs. Steam or grill asparagus spears to desired level of doneness. In a small saucepan place remaining lemon marinade along with lemon rind, ½ cup water, and spices, and cook until pulp starts to come out. You may add a little Stevia if you wish for added sweetness. Reduce liquid by half. Remove lemon rind and pour over grilled asparagus. Garnish with lemon wedges and salt and pepper to taste.

HCG DIET Tip *Experiment with different varieties of vegetables in the recipes such as Chinese, Napa, and Savoy cabbage or different varieties of tomatoes such as Roma, Heirloom, and grape tomatoes.*

Roasted Fruit and Vegetable Kabobs

Ingredients
1 apple, cut into large chunks
¼ onion, cut into 1 inch petals
1 tomato, cut into chunks
1 tablespoon apple cider vinegar
1 tablespoon lemon juice
½ teaspoon mint leaves, crushed
½ teaspoon cilantro leaves, crushed
Pinch of allspice
Stevia to taste

Makes 1 serving
(1 fruit, 1 vegetable)

2 grams protein

0 fat

135 calories

> Marinate fruit and vegetables in lemon juice and vinegar with Stevia and spices in the refrigerator for 20 minutes or more. Soak wooden skewers in water for five minutes. Layer chopped apple, onion petals, and tomato alternately on skewers. Place on grill for 5-8 minutes or until desired level of doneness. Top with herbs and serve with lemon wedges.

Hot Pickled Red Cabbage

Ingredients
1 ½ cups red cabbage, chopped
1 apple, diced
½ cup apple cider vinegar
¼ cup water
2 tablespoons Bragg's liquid aminos
2 tablespoons red onion, chopped
1 clove garlic, crushed and minced
A pinch of red pepper flakes
Salt and pepper to taste

Makes 2 serving
(1 vegetable, 1 fruit)

2 grams protein

0 fat

145 calories

> Slow cook cabbage and apples in water and apple cider vinegar. Add spices, chopped onion, garlic, and Stevia. Add salt and pepper to taste. Serve hot or cold.

Fennel with Herbs

Ingredients
1 ½ cups fennel bulbs, diced
½ cup vegetable broth or water
2 tablespoons lemon juice
Your choice of marinade or dressing (See **Dressings, Sauces, and Marinades** section for ideas)

Thoroughly wash and trim fresh fennel. Cook the fennel for several minutes in a little water or vegetable broth adding pepper, lemon, salt, and fresh or dried herbs. Try Italian style or toss with Cajun spiced. Cook until the bulb portion is tender and delicious. Fennel may also be grilled on the barbeque.

Makes 1 or more servings (1 vegetable)

1 gram protein

0 fat

45 calories

PHASE 3 MODIFICATIONS: Drizzle with melted butter or olive oil. Fennel has a slight licorice taste and goes well with fish.

Hot Peppered Chicory

Ingredients
1 cup chicory, minced
Salt and pepper to taste
2 tablespoons lemon juice
¼ cup vegetable broth or water

Mince the chicory. In a small saucepan add chicory to broth and add lemon juice, salt, and pepper. Cook for 3-5 minutes and serve hot.

Makes 1 or more servings (1 vegetable)

1 gram protein

0 fat

20 calories

PHASE 3 MODIFICATIONS: Add a little butter or olive oil or omit the lemon juice and add a small amount of half and half or cream cheese. Top with grated parmesan cheese or mix in crumbled feta cheese.

Herbed Asparagus

Ingredients
5 spears asparagus
½ cup vegetable, chicken broth, or water
2 tablespoons lemon juice
1 clove of garlic, crushed and minced
1 tablespoon onion, minced
1 teaspoon Italian herb mix
Water as needed

Lightly sauté onion, garlic, and herbs in the chicken broth for about one minute. Add the asparagus and cook until tender. Top with herbed sauce (add a little powdered garlic and onion for a thicker sauce). Garnish with parsley and lemon wedges.

Makes 1 or more servings
(1 vegetable)
5 grams protein
0 fat
65 calories

PHASE 3 MODIFICATIONS: Add a splash of white wine. Stir in cold cubes of butter whisking gently to create a butter sauce or omit the lemon juice and stir in ¼ cup cream or half and half. Add a few capers and top with fresh herbs.

Roasted Tomato with Onion

Ingredients
4 thin whole slices of onion
4 thick cut tomato slices
1-2 cloves of garlic, sliced
2 leaves fresh basil, rolled and sliced
Sprinkle of dried or fresh oregano
Salt and black pepper to taste
Stevia to taste (optional)
Squeeze of lemon juice

Lay out thin slices of onion on a baking sheet. Salt and pepper the onion and sprinkle with lemon juice. Lay a few slices of basil and garlic on top of the onion. Top onion slices with a slice of tomato. Top the tomato with remaining basil and garlic. Bake at 375 degrees for 10-15 minutes or until desired level of doneness. Sprinkle with lemon juice and salt and pepper to taste.

Makes 4 servings
(1 vegetable)
3 grams protein
0 fat
55 calories

HCG DIET Tip
Buy live herb plants like basil, rosemary, mint, oregano, and parsley plants, etc. You can grow your own herb garden for fresh flavors at your fingertips.

Spiced Beet Greens (substitute spinach)

Ingredients
1 ½ cups beet greens
¼ cup chicken broth or water
4 tablespoons lemon juice
2 cloves of garlic, crushed and minced
¼ teaspoon paprika
Pinch of cumin
Pinch of lemon zest
Salt and pepper to taste

Makes 1 serving
(1 vegetable)

1 gram protein

0 fat

30 calories

PHASE 3
MODIFICATIONS: Top
with 1 tablespoon of
crushed pecans.

▶ Combine spices in liquid ingredients. Lightly sauté beet greens in spice mixture. Serve hot and garnish with lemon and fresh ground black pepper.

Chilled Pesto Tomato Salad

Ingredients
2 medium tomatoes or 3 Roma tomatoes, sliced
3 leaves of fresh basil, rolled and sliced
1 slice **Savory Red Onion** or **Caramelized Onion Garnish** (optional)
1-2 cloves of garlic, minced
2 tablespoons lemon juice
2 tablespoons caper juice
1 tablespoon of apple cider vinegar

1-2 servings
(1 vegetable)

3 grams protein

0 fat

65 calories

PHASE 3
MODIFICATIONS: Layer
sliced tomatoes with
fresh mozzarella cheese
to make a Caprese salad.
Brush with olive oil.

▶ Toss fresh tomatoes with spices and vinegar and coat completely. Marinate for at least 1 hour. Top with onion garnish and serve.

Strawberry Sorbet/Pops

Ingredients
4-6 medium strawberries
Approximately 3 cubes of ice
Any powdered or flavored Stevia to taste
½ teaspoon vanilla powder or cocoa (optional)
2 tablespoons lemon juice
¼ cup water

▶ Blend ingredients together until smooth. Pour into a dish or Popsicle molds and freeze until firm.

Makes 1 serving
(1 fruit)

.5 grams protein

0 fat

35 calories

PHASE 3
MODIFICATIONS: Add half and half or cream and whipped egg whites. Mix in chopped nuts and freeze for an ice cream style dessert.

Orange or Lemon Pops

Ingredients
Juice of ½ lemon or 1 small orange, juiced
Powdered Stevia to taste

▶ Mix Stevia to taste into lemon or orange juice. Pour into Popsicle molds and freeze.

Makes one serving
(1 fruit)

0 protein

0 fat

15 calories (lemon)
50 calories (orange)

Apple Chips

Ingredients
1 apple
Dash of cinnamon
Stevia to taste

▶ Slice apples thinly, coat with Stevia and cinnamon. Place in a dehydrator or bake at 325 degrees until chewy and a little crispy.

Makes 1 serving
(1 fruit)

.5 grams protein

0 fat

85 calories

Apple Cookies

Ingredients
Pulp from 1 apple
1/8 teaspoon cinnamon
Pinch of nutmeg
1/8 teaspoon vanilla powder
Stevia to taste
1 tablespoon lemon juice

> Mix pulp from 1 apple (use juice for a virgin apple martini). Mix with Stevia and spices and form into cookies (1-2). Bake the cookies for approximately 15-20 minutes or until slightly brown.

Makes 1 serving
(1 fruit)

.5 gram protein

0 fat

45 calories

PHASE 3
MODIFICATIONS: Add chopped walnuts or pecan meal and a little butter to the apple mixture, then bake.

Iced and Spiced Orange Slices

Ingredients
1 orange, sliced or segmented
2 tablespoons lemon juice
¼ teaspoon cinnamon
¼ teaspoon powdered vanilla
Pinch of nutmeg to taste
Pinch of powdered clove to taste
Pinch of cardamom to taste
Powdered Stevia to taste

> Mix powdered spices and Stevia together. Dip orange slices in lemon juice and dredge with spice mixture. Freeze until firm.

Variations: Substitute strawberry or apple slices.

Makes 1 serving
(1 fruit)

1 gram protein

0 fat

65 calories

HCG DIET Tip *Try some of the flavored varieties of liquid Stevia for when you want something sweet. Enjoy with fresh fruit, coffee, or tea. Vanilla, dark chocolate, English toffee, peppermint, orange, and other flavors are available. Check your local health food store or shop online for additional flavor options.*

Apple Slices with Cinnamon Sauce

Ingredients
1 apple, sliced
3 tablespoons lemon juice
1 teaspoon apple cider vinegar
1 teaspoon cinnamon
Dash of nutmeg
Powdered Stevia to taste

▷ In the microwave or small saucepan heat the liquid and spice ingredients together, stirring constantly. Serve in a small dipping bowl with chilled apple slices or other fruit.

Makes 1 serving
(1 fruit)

.5 gram protein

0 fat

90 calories

PHASE 3
MODIFICATIONS:
Dissolve spices in lemon juice. Whisk in small cubes of cold butter to make a sauce. Add rum extract or vanilla. Sauté apple slices in spiced butter mixture.

Fruit with Warm Vanilla Sauce

Ingredients
Your choice of allowed fruit
1 tablespoon vanilla powder
2 tablespoons lemon juice
½ teaspoon apple cider vinegar
Powdered Stevia to taste

▷ In a small saucepan or dipping bowl stir Stevia and vanilla powder into lemon juice and vinegar. Heat the sauce on the stove or in the microwave. Pour into a dipping bowl. Dip fresh fruit into the warm sauce and enjoy.

Makes 1 serving
(1 fruit)

1 gram protein

0 fat

100 calories (apple)
60 calories (grapefruit)
40 calories (strawberries)
75 calories (orange)

PHASE 3
MODIFICATIONS: Stir in 1 tablespoon of cold butter cut into small cubes and whisk quickly until blended. Or add a small amount of cream and omit the lemon juice. Add a little cinnamon or rum extract for added flavor.

Caramel Apple Pie

Ingredients
1 apple
1 tablespoon lemon juice
1 tablespoon water
1 teaspoon apple cider vinegar
1 packet powdered Stevia
1 teaspoon ground cinnamon
Pinch of nutmeg
1 tablespoon water
English toffee Stevia to taste

Makes 1 serving
(1 fruit)

.5 gram protein

0 fat

95 calories

PHASE 3
MODIFICATIONS: Add a
small amount of melted
butter to the mixture and
top with a tablespoon
of chopped walnuts or
pecans.

Slice apple into very thin slices. Arrange in layers in a round 3 inch crème Brulee dish. For each layer, sprinkle generously with cinnamon, nutmeg, and powdered and English toffee Stevia. Continue layering with spices until dish is full. Sprinkle lemon juice, apple cider vinegar, and water over the apple slices. Bake at 375 degrees for approximately 20-25 minutes or until apples are cooked and top is slightly crispy. Drizzle with additional English toffee Stevia if desired. Serve warm.

Warm Spiced Oranges

Ingredients
One orange, sliced or segmented
2 tablespoons lemon juice
1/8 teaspoon ground cinnamon
Dash of cloves
Dash of nutmeg
1/8 teaspoon powdered vanilla
Stevia to taste (powdered or flavored liquid)

Makes 1 serving
(1 fruit)

1 gram protein

0 fat

70 calories

Mix spices with lemon juice and Stevia. Warm slightly in saucepan and add oranges. Cook for 2-3 minutes. Serve hot or chilled.

HCG
DIET
Tip *Freeze fresh fruits like strawberries, grapefruits or oranges to puree with ice and make smoothies or frozen desserts.*

Frozen Grapefruit Spears

Ingredients
½ grapefruit in slices or segments
2 tablespoons lemon juice
Pinch of lemon zest
Powdered Stevia to taste

Makes 1 serving
(1 fruit)
1 gram protein
0 fat
50 calories

▶ Dip grapefruit chunks in lemon juice and coat with Stevia and lemon zest. Freeze until firm and enjoy as an icy treat.

Iced Cocoa Strawberries

Ingredients
4-6 medium strawberries
1 tablespoon dry defatted cocoa
Powdered Stevia to taste

Makes 1 serving
(1 fruit)
.5 gram protein
0 fat
35 calories

▶ Mix cocoa and Stevia together. Slice strawberries and dip in cocoa mixture. Place on wax or parchment paper and freeze until firm. Variations: Use orange segments.

Warm Strawberry Compote

Ingredients
5 large fresh sliced strawberries
2 tablespoons lemon juice
Dash of cinnamon
Dash of nutmeg
Dash of cayenne
Dash of salt
Vanilla or dark chocolate Stevia to taste

Makes 1 serving
(1 fruit)
.5 gram protein
0 fat
35 calories

Phase 3 modifications: Omit the lemon juice and stir in 2 tablespoons cream cheese or heavy cream. Top with chopped roasted nuts.

▶ In a small saucepan, combine ingredients and stir thoroughly. Sauté on medium heat until warm and bubbly and a sauce develops. Serve warm in a bowl. Garnish with mint. Top with cinnamon **Melba Croutons**.

Applesauce with Cinnamon

Ingredients
1 apple
½ teaspoon cinnamon
Pinch of nutmeg
Powdered Stevia to taste

Makes 1 serving
(1 fruit)
.5 gram protein
0 fat
95 calories

▶ Peel and puree apple in a food processor. Add in cinnamon and Stevia to taste. Serve chilled.

Dark Chocolate Flavored Strawberry or Orange Slices

Ingredients
1 orange, peeled and sliced or handful of strawberries, sliced
Dark chocolate Stevia extract

Makes 1 serving
(1 fruit)
1 gram protein
0 fat
65 calories (orange)
30 calories (strawberries)

▶ Arrange orange or strawberry slices in a bowl. Drizzle dark chocolate Stevia over the slices and serve chilled. Garnish with mint if desired.

HCG DIET *Tips*

- *Enjoy small amounts of defatted cocoa and dry unsweetened vanilla powder as a "spice" in some of my recipes. Defatted cocoa and vanilla powder may have trace amounts of fat or starch in them and should be used sparingly. Always monitor your weight when using these items and discontinue if you feel it is stalling your weight loss.*

- *Avoid artificial sweeteners such as Aspartame, sucralose, and saccharine completely as they are toxic chemicals which can actually contribute to weight issues as well as being linked to many other health problems. I personally recommend Stevia as the sweetener of choice for this diet and for life. Stevia is an all natural herb that is zero calories, up to 300 times sweeter than sugar, and will not affect your blood sugar levels or your weight loss.*

Strawberry Smoothie

Ingredients
5 large frozen strawberries
Flavored or powdered Stevia (try vanilla or milk chocolate liquid Stevia)
1 tablespoon milk (optional)
Ice cubes

▶ Blend together and serve in a tall glass. Garnish with a strawberry, lemon slice or mint leaf garnish if desired.

Makes 1 serving
(1 fruit)

.5 gram protein

0 fat

30 calories

PHASE 3
MODIFICATIONS: Mix
in a little half and half,
cream, or quality protein
powder. Add peaches,
fresh raspberries,
or make mixed fruit
smoothies.

Iced Tea

Ingredients
Your choice of tea:
  Green
  Yerba mate
  Chamomile
  Mint
  Fruit flavored
  Chai spice
  Cranberry
Stevia to taste
6 ounces of hot water per serving

▶ Brew your choice of tea in hot water. Brew the tea a little strong. Chill in the refrigerator and then serve over ice or mix with 3 ounces of sparkling mineral water to make a soda. Add Stevia to taste and garnish with mint leaves or lemon slices.

Makes 1 serving

0 calories

HCG DIET Tip

Keep bags of tea in your bag, pocket, or car for on the go drinks or to take to restaurants. Add hot water for hot tea, or carry iced versions of the recommended teas in a cooler or chiller bottle. You can use these to flavor your iced tea or make your own homemade lemonade by asking the waiter for a plate of lemon wedges on the side.

Chocolate Toffee Coffee Smoothie

Ingredients
6 ounces strong brewed coffee
English toffee flavored Stevia to taste
Dark or milk chocolate Stevia to taste
¼ teaspoon defatted powdered cocoa (Wondercocoa)
Ice cubes
1 tablespoon milk (optional)

▷ Puree ingredients together. Add ice, Stevia, and milk.

Makes 1 serving
less than 10 calories

PHASE 3
MODIFICATIONS:
Add half and half or
cream and blend. Make
homemade Stevia
sweetened ice cream
style dessert by adding
whipped egg whites,
whipped cream, Stevia,
and cocoa. Freeze and
enjoy.

Strawberry Lemonade

Ingredients
2 strawberries, mashed or pureed
Juice of ¼ lemon
Stevia to taste
8 ounces water (plain or sparkling mineral water)

▷ Mix lemon juice and pureed strawberries in a glass. Pour over ice and sweeten with Stevia.

Makes 1 serving
(1 fruit)

0 protein

0 fat

15 calories

HCG
DIET
Tip
*Make your own
homemade
sparkling sodas or
other mixed drinks
with allowed fruit
juice and sparkling
mineral water. See
recipes for flavor
ideas. Serve them
in a martini glass
with a wedge of
lemon or other
garnish and enjoy.*

Refreshing Grapefruit Virgin Martini

Ingredients
Juice of ½ grapefruit
5 ounces sparkling mineral water
Ice
Vanilla Stevia to taste

▸ Mix juice with Stevia and pour over ice. Add sparkling mineral water and enjoy.

Makes 1 serving
(1 fruit)

1 gram protein

0 fat

45 calories

PHASE 3
MODIFICATIONS: Add 1
shot of vodka.

Sparkling Virgin Apple Martini/Caramel Apple Martini

Ingredients
1 apple, juiced (use pulp for **Meatloaf** or **Apple Cookies**)
6 ounces chilled sparkling mineral water
2 tablespoons lemon juice
Vanilla or English toffee liquid Stevia
Apple slice for garnish
Crushed ice (optional)

▸ Combine apple and lemon juices with flavored Stevia. Add sparkling mineral water and ice if desired. Serve in a martini glass with a slice or curl of apple peel for garnish. Works great with tangy apples like granny smith or for a sweeter apple tini you can use red delicious or other sweet apple.

Variation: For a **Caramel Apple Martini**, add a little English toffee Stevia instead of vanilla.

Makes 1 serving
(1 fruit)

0 protein

0 fat

45 calories

PHASE 3
MODIFICATIONS: Add 1
shot of vodka.

HCG DIET *Tip*
Serve your iced tea, lemonade, or other beverages in a fancy glass like a martini glass when at a party or out to dinner. Garnish with lemon, mint, or a slice or two of strawberry. No one will know you aren't imbibing and that you are on a diet.

Bloody Hot Thin Mary

Ingredients
8 ounces fresh tomato juice
1 tablespoon apple cider vinegar
Cayenne pepper to taste
2 tablespoons lemon juice
1 teaspoon hot sauce
Celery salt
Freshly ground black pepper
3 dashes of Worcestershire sauce

Makes 1 serving
(1 vegetable)

.5 gram protein

0 fat

35 calories

PHASE 3
MODIFICATIONS: Add 1
shot of vodka.

▶ Add all spices to fresh tomato juice. Stir well and serve over ice. Serve
with freshly ground black pepper.

Variation: Add ¼ teaspoon horseradish.

Hot Apple Cider

Ingredients
1 apple, juiced
2 tablespoons lemon juice
1 teaspoon apple cider vinegar
¼ teaspoon cinnamon
Pinch of nutmeg
Pinch of allspice
Pinch of clove
Pinch of lemon zest
Stevia to taste
Water

Makes 1 serving
(1 fruit)

.5 gram protein

0 fat

75 calories

▶ Heat the juice with spices and a little water in a small saucepan. Serve
hot with a cinnamon stick.

HCG DIET Tip *Add cinnamon to coffee grounds for a wonderful flavored coffee. Cinnamon is a healthful spice that is believed to help decrease blood sugar levels. It tastes wonderful with fruits and adds spice to chicken and vegetable dishes.*

Lemon or Strawberry Ice Cubes

Ingredients
4-6 strawberries or 1 lemon, juiced
¼ cup water
Mint, chopped (optional)
Stevia to taste (optional)

Makes 1 serving
(1 fruit)

.5 gram protein

0 fat

15 calories (lemon)
30 calories (strawberries)

▶ Puree strawberries with water and Stevia or juice lemon and mix with
water and mint. Pour fresh juice of lemons or pureed strawberries
into ice cube trays and freeze. Add to cold drinks, recipes, and teas for
added flavor.

Mint Chocolate Coffee Smoothie

Ingredients
6 ounces strong brewed coffee, chilled
Peppermint Stevia
Dark or milk chocolate Stevia
¼ teaspoon defatted powdered cocoa (Wondercocoa)
Ice cubes
1 tablespoon milk (optional)

Makes 1 serving
less than 10 calories

PHASE 3
MODIFICATIONS: Add
half and half or cream.

▶ Blend ingredients together until smooth. Serve with a mint leaf
garnish.

Lemonade

Ingredients
Juice of ½ lemon
Stevia to taste
8 ounces water (plain or sparkling mineral water)

Makes 1 serving
less than 10 calories

▶ Squeeze lemon juice into a glass. Add rind of the lemon, Stevia and ice.

HCG
DIET
Tip
Carry packets of powdered Stevia in your bag or pocket when dining out at restaurants.

Virgin Sparkling Mojito

Ingredients
Fresh mint leaves, crushed
Juice of ½ lime or lemon
Peppermint or plain powdered Stevia
6 ounces sparkling mineral water
Crushed ice

Makes 1 serving
less than 10 calories

PHASE 3
MODIFICATIONS: Add 1
shot of rum.

▶ Crush mint leaves to release the flavor. Add liquid or powdered Stevia and lemon or lime juice. Add sparkling mineral water and crushed ice. Top with a sprig of mint and enjoy.

Apple Green Tea Sparkler

Ingredients
1 apple, juiced
½ cup brewed green tea, chilled
¼ cup sparkling mineral water
1 teaspoon vanilla Stevia
Pinch of cinnamon

Makes 1 serving
(1 fruit)
0 protein
0 fat
60 calories

▶ Combine juice of 1 apple, green tea, cinnamon, vanilla Stevia together. Add crushed ice and sparkling mineral water. Garnish with apple curls and lemon wedge.

HCG DIET Tip

Mix teas such as green tea, mint, or vanilla Yerba Mate together to make a new flavor. Brew very strong and serve over ice with lemon slices and Stevia for a cool treat during the summer. You can also make them into ice pops in your freezer for a refreshing dessert treat.

Sparkling Chocolate Mint Coffee Soda

Ingredients
4 ounces strong brewed coffee
4 ounces sparkling mineral water
Dark chocolate or milk chocolate Stevia
Peppermint Stevia to taste
1 tablespoon milk (optional)
Ice
Mint leaves (optional)

Makes 1 serving
less than 10 calories

▶ Mix coffee, Stevia, and milk. Pour over ice and add sparkling mineral water. Garnish with mint leaf.

Homemade Diet Soda

Ingredients
8 ounces sparkling mineral water
Flavored Stevia to taste
Your choice of 3-5 tablespoons fresh orange, lemon, or apple juice
(optional)

Makes 1 serving
0 calories when prepared with Stevia

▶ Add flavored Stevia to sparkling mineral water to taste. The most commonly available options are orange, grape, vanilla, chocolate, and root beer. There are many flavors of Stevia on the market. Shop at your local health food store or online to find additional flavors. Add fresh lemon or lime juices and slices to make a lemon lime flavor. Get creative. Try combining flavors like orange and vanilla to create a dreamsicle soda.

HCG DIET *Tip* *Enjoy drinking healthful teas such as Yerba Mate, Green, Oolong, and herbal teas such as Chamomile. These teas have been shown to decrease hunger pangs particularly in the first week of eating the VLCD/500 calorie diet. They may also increase the metabolism and assist the fat burning process.*

Update
ON THE AUTHOR

Hello everyone. I'm thrilled to report that that I'm happily maintaining my weight and wearing a slim size 4-6 over 2 years after the HCG Diet! I've lost inches all over, particularly in my waist and thighs and nearly 60 pounds total. It is such a thrill to shop in the "small/medium" section when I go to the store.

It feels absolutely incredible to no longer feel like a slave to food or my weight. The yo-yo dieting, food cravings, and impossibly low metabolism are now a thing of the past and I know that with my new and healthier style of eating, and faster, more efficient metabolism, I no longer have to worry about my weight. This truly is the ultimate, miracle, weight loss solution I have searched for all of my life. Good luck to you all in your own weight loss journey.

I wish you all the success in the world as you begin this amazing journey of transformation. I am sure that you will have as much success as I have experienced as you go through this process and meet your weight loss goals. Your life is about to change!

Wishing you all the best,

Tammy Skye

Tammy Skye

---

*Faith is taking the first step
even when you don't see the whole staircase.*

— MARTIN LUTHER KING JR.

More HCG Diet Gourmet Recipes — 150 More Delicious, Low Calorie Recipes for the HCG Diet

Enjoy these easy and delicious recipes during the "HCG Phase" (also known as Phase 2 or P2) while you lose weight with the HCG Diet.

The HCG Diet Gourmet Cookbook, the "Stabilizing Phase" (also known as Phase 3 or P3) Starch and Sugar Free Recipes to Help You Reset Your Metabolism and Stabilize Your Weight Loss

Enjoy these delicious Phase 3 stabilizing recipes to help you manage your weight and reset your metabolism. Featuring, a wide variety of starch and sugar free entrees, appetizers, soups and salads, and decadent desserts as you transition to Phase 3 of the HCG Diet.

www.hcgrecipes.com

Visit the HCG Diet Gourmet Cookbook blog for more HCG Diet tips, health and wellness info, and recipes at www.hcgrecipes.com/blog

The Fibernoodle Cookbook

Featuring the amazing, calorie free, pure fiber, Shirataki noodles from Japan. These delicious recipes feature many homestyle favorites, Italian pasta recipes, Asian noodle dishes and more. The recipes are prepared without sugar or starch and are easily adapted to the "Stabilizing Phase" (also known as Phase 3 or P3) of the HCG Diet.

www.fibernoodlecookbook.com

The Coffee, Tea, Sugar Free Cookbook

Featuring delicious specialty coffee and tea drink recipes using all natural Stevia

www.coffeeteasugarfree.com

HCG Diet Stories

Inspiring true stories of real HCG Dieters

www.hcgdietstories.com

**Sign up to be on the list for a
big discount as soon as these books are released.**

info@hcgrecipes.com

RESOURCES AND LINKS

RECOMMENDED READING

Pounds and Inches a New Approach to Obesity

The original HCG Diet program and book by Dr. A.T.W. Simeons.

The Weight Loss Cure They Don't Want You to Know About

The revolutionary book by Kevin Trudeau that discusses the HCG Diet in detail with additional nutrition and wellness recommendations for healthy living.

www.naturalcures.com (can be purchased at most bookstores)

HCG Diet Made Simple

An invaluable guide for HCG Dieters by Harmony Clearwater Grace that offers step by step advice and a wealth of valuable information and resources to help you lose weight and be successful with the HCG Diet.

www.hcgdietmadesimplebook.com

Living the Sweet Life the Sugar Free Way

A groundbreaking book by Barbara Gibson about how to break free from sugar addiction and have better health, reduced cravings, and more energy.

www.freefromsugar.com

RECOMMENDED PRODUCTS AND

SERVICES

My Sweet Stevia

A website that offers a wide selection of the Stevia products featured in this book as well as sugar and calorie free Cappella flavor drops.

www.mysweetstevia.com

HCG Supplies

A trusted supplier of complete HCG Diet supply kits. Free phone and email support, free shipping and excellent customer service.

www.hcgsupplies.net

Miracle Noodles

The amazing, calorie free, pure fiber, Shirataki noodles compatible with the "No Starch/No Sugar" Stabilizing Phase 3 of the HCG Diet.

www.miraclenoodles.net

The HCG Recipes App

Our very own online application of these recipes and other helpful weight loss tools like a calorie counter, journal, weight tracker and more! Use it on the web or from your phone.

www.hcgrecipesapp.com

Notes